1973-1977 YACHT RACING RULES AND TACTICS

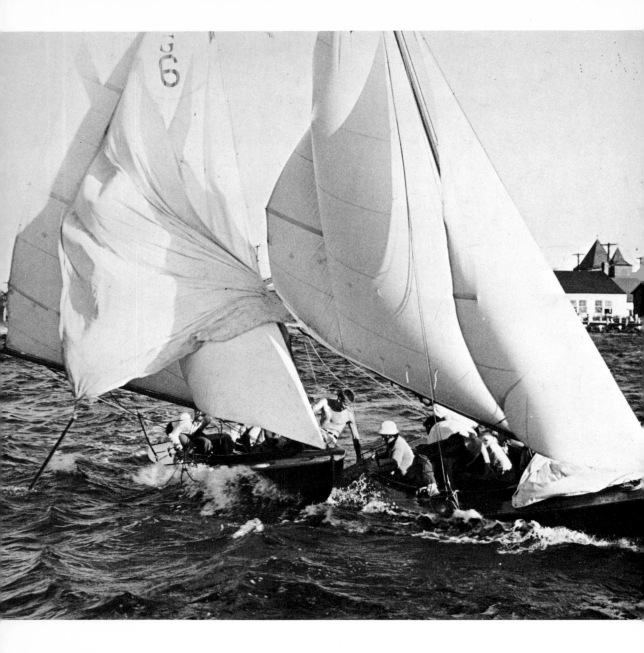

The "Sailing Rules When Yachts Meet" are designed to avoid collisions. Read new rule 67, which provides that when there is contact between two yachts and neither of them retires nor protests, both shall be disqualified.

1973-1977 YACHT RACING RULES AND TACTICS

7TH EDITION

GORDON C. AYMAR

Diagram Photographs by the Author

VNR VAN NOSTRAND REINHOLD COMPANY
NEW YORK CINCINNATI LONDON TORONTO MELBOURNE

List of Photographers

Here are the photographers whose action pictures have added so much to this book. For every hundred yacht photographs one may be good. For there are many elements that go to make up the good one. Perhaps you have a choppy sea and not enough light, or sun and an uninteresting sea. Or perfect wind and sea and sun and you're too far away. Perhaps you are near and the conditions are perfect but there is no competitive situation. You are torn between getting depth of focus on the one hand and speed on the other.

One of the best men in the business has told me that the cream of his pictures is taken on perhaps one day a year, and for the top he has to go back to a certain squally day in 1932.

Action photographs are from the following sources: Acme; Ray Chapin; James D. Foley; Lew Hahn; Keystone View Co.; H. Marth; Morris Rosenfeld; W. C. Sawyer; Underwood & Underwood; Wide World Photos, Inc.

The diagrams and diagram photographs of models were made by the author.

Jacket Photograph by Stan Rosenfeld

Van Nostrand Reinhold Company Regional Offices:
New York Cincinnati Chicago Millbrae Dallas

Van Nostrand Reinhold Company Foreign Offices:
London Toronto Melbourne

Library of Congress Catalog Card Number: 73–110056

Published simultaneously in Canada by
Van Nostrand Reinhold Ltd.

Published by Van Nostrand Reinhold Company
450 West 33rd Street, New York, N.Y. 10001

10 9 8 7 6 5 4 3 2 1

Library of Congress Cataloging in Publication Data

Aymar, Gordon Christian, 1893-
    1973-1977 yacht racing rules and tactics.

    First (1936)-3d (1948) ed. published under title:
A pictorial primer of yacht racing & tactics;
4th (1954)-6th (1970) ed: Yacht racing rules & tactics.
    1. Yacht racing—Rules. I. Title. II. Title:
Yacht racing rules and tactics.
GV826.7.A95 1974   797.1'4   73-23094
ISBN 0-442-20388-8

CONTENTS

PART ONE: THE RACING RULES

DEFINITIONS: N.A.Y.R.U. Rules, Part I 3

SAILING RULES WHEN YACHTS MEET:
N.A.Y.R.U. Rules, Part IV 10

PART TWO: RACING TACTICS

INTRODUCTION

"One picture is worth ten thousand words." So the Chinese concluded thousands of years ago. And there is still gunpowder in those words today. From the caveman's first drawing to the latest TV show, pictures have been the quickest and simplest way of imparting an idea.

When a yachtsman attempts to describe how he was approaching the starting line on such-and-such a tack, when a so-and-so came barging down upon him to windward, he generally uses both hands and a couple of match sticks. He would show you a movie of it if he could, yet even a movie, taken at eye level, would not show clearly the angles at which the yachts approached each other. It would take a bird's-eye view to do that—a view reserved exclusively for aviators and the God of Yachtsmen.

It is not to be expected that anyone will learn how to race from reading this book. There is no substitute for practical experience. If tactics alone could win a race, there would be no reason for considering the set of sails, the condition of the hull and rigging, the action of currents, the peculiar behavior of winds and the many factors which go toward making racing so engagingly complicated.

For the young, let me say that the rules were invented to keep people out of trouble with their competitors; tactics were invented to make as much trouble for them as possible. The two should not be confused. Don't use a knowledge of the rules as an offensive weapon; win races by sailing, not by protests. But don't forget that "ignorance of the rules is no excuse," as the Appeals Committee of the N.A.Y.R.U. so aptly puts it in the decision in Appeal No. 38.

Yachting is a sport for gentlemen, not as distinguished from ladies, but as distinguished from the unsportsmanlike. Rule 49—Fair Sailing says, "A yacht shall attempt to win a race only by fair sailing and superior speed and skill . . ." She may be disqualified before or after racing if she seriously hinders a yacht which is racing. Whatever rule applies, if she makes no attempt to avoid a collision which results in serious damage, she may be disqualified. She should withdraw from a race immediately if she knows she has sinned. Even though she has the right of way, she must not so alter course as to prevent the other yacht from keeping clear. She should hail a yacht even though it does not have the right of way, when she alters course in a way which may not be foreseen by the other yacht.* This kind of sportsmanlike behavior is covered by "rules which always apply." An indication that the authorities are concerned with this appears in rule 74.3: "After a gross breach of good manners or sportsmanship the Race Committee may exclude a competitor from further participation in a series or take other disciplinary action."

I wish to take this opportunity to pay my respects to the North American Yacht Racing Union for the fine work they have done over the years, and to thank them for their permission to print the rules in full; without these the book would be incomplete.

South Kent, Connecticut

* Except when luffing under Rule 38.1.

WARNING

The rules illustrated in the following pages are The Racing Rules of the International Yacht Racing Union as adopted by the North American Yacht Racing Union, Part I—Definitions, and Part IV—Sailing Rules When Yachts Meet. These are the parts which gain from illustration. They do not represent all the rules, which, with the Appendices, are printed in full on pages 41-83. This entire text must be read if one is to be completely informed.

In translating and interpreting these rules, it shall be understood that the word "shall" is mandatory, whereas the word "should" is directive and not mandatory, and the words "can" and "may" are permissive.

Parts I and IV are now identical all over the world. Of all the other rules, the N.A.Y.R.U. has exercised its right to alter only eight, and has added only three of its own.

In the following diagram photographs, the WHITE yacht is always in the right or winning; the BLACK is always in the wrong, vulnerable or losing.

In the following text direct quotations from the N.A.Y.R.U. Rules are in a serif type, and the author's comments are in a sans serif type. Except for the complete text of the rules beginning on page 41, quotations from the rules are also set within prominent quotation marks, as below:

" The rules of Part IV do not apply in any way to a vessel which is neither intending to race nor racing; such vessel shall be treated in accordance with the International Regulations for Preventing Collisions at Sea or Government Right-of-Way Rules applicable to the area concerned. "

" 1973 **Changes:** As in 1969, the 1973 rules include a good many small changes for consistency and better understanding.

Rules 22.3, 67, 74.3 and Appendix 3 are new. So also, but of different application, are Appendices 4 and 5.

Without implying that other changes need not be examined, attention is called to rules 32, 34, 35, 40, 42.1 (a) (ii), 52.2, 73.2 (b), the team racing rules and Appendix 6.

For ready comparison most changes, even when only the number of the rule, are indicated by a vertical line in the left margin. "

THE RACING RULES

PART ONE

According to the Definitions, the yacht in the background is the leeward yacht; the one in the foreground is the windward yacht, since they are both on the same tack and neither is clear astern of the other.

2

DEFINITIONS: N.A.Y.R.U. Rules, Part I

When a term defined in Part I is used in its defined sense it is printed in **bold** *type. All definitions and italicized notes rank as rules.*

"Racing—A yacht is **racing** from her preparatory signal until she has either **finished** and cleared the finishing line and finishing **marks** or retired, or until the race has been **cancelled, postponed** or **abandoned,** except that in match or team races, the sailing instructions may prescribe that a yacht is **racing** from any specified time before the preparatory signal. **"**

Notice that a yacht is "racing" until she has "cleared the finishing line and finishing **marks."** Avoid fouling any racing yacht or the Committee Boat right after you finish. Also notice the provision that in match or team races, the sailing instructions may prescribe that a yacht is racing *"from any specified time before the preparatory signal."*

"Starting—A yacht **starts** when, after fulfilling her penalty obligations, if any, under rule 51.1 (c), Sailing the Course, and after her starting signal, any part of her hull, crew or equipment first crosses the starting line in the direction of the course to the first **mark. "**

"Finishing —A yacht **finishes** when any part of her hull, or of her crew or equipment in normal position, crosses the finishing line from the direction of the course from the last **mark,**[*] after fulfilling her penalty obligations, if any, under rule 52.2, Touching a Mark. **"**

Notice that it is any part of her hull, *crew* or equipment which determines starting and finishing. Don't let your crew lean out over the bow to try to beat a boat at the finish. He must remain "in normal position."

The spinnaker on this yacht has crossed the finishing line. She therefore qualifies as having finished. (See **starting** above, also.) Rule 51.5 states: "It is not necessary for a yacht to cross the finishing line completely. After **finishing** she may clear it in either direction."

[*] Appeal No. 84 states: "We rule that 'the last mark' means the last turning mark prior to the finishing line."

A is starting and finishing mark. C is Committee Boat (which shifts position to set up finishing line).

It is customary to lay out a course so that all marks are left on the same hand. If there is no specific mention to the contrary in the Sailing Instructions, leave all marks on the same hand as the starting mark. However, even if the Committee Boat is anchored on the side of the starting or finishing mark opposite to that prescribed in the Sailing Instructions, "a yacht shall start and finish only as prescribed in the starting and finishing definitions."*

" **Luffing**—Altering course towards the wind until head to wind.

" **Tacking**—A yacht is **tacking** from the moment she is beyond head to wind until she has **borne away**, if beating to windward, to a **close-hauled** course; if not beating to windward, to the course on which her mainsail has filled. "

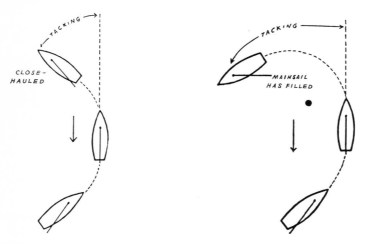

(In actual practice, a well-sailed yacht will always fill her mainsail sooner than shown in the right hand diagram.)

* Rule 51.1(a).

4

Bearing Away—Altering course away from the wind until a yacht begins to **jibe.**

Jibing—A yacht begins to **jibe** at the moment when, with the wind aft, the foot of her mainsail crosses her center line and completes the **jibe** when the mainsail has filled on the other **tack.**

On a Tack—A yacht is **on a tack** except when she is **tacking** or **jibing.** A yacht is on the **tack** (starboard or port) corresponding to her **windward** side.

Close-hauled—A yacht is **close-hauled** when sailing by the wind as close as she can lie with advantage in working to windward.

Leeward and **Windward**—The **leeward** side of a yacht is that on which she is, or, if **luffing** head to wind, was, carrying her mainsail. The opposite is the **windward** side.

When neither of two yachts on the same **tack** is **clear astern,** the one on the **leeward** side of the other is the **leeward yacht.** The other is the **windward yacht.**"

"**Clear Astern** and **Clear Ahead; Overlap**—A yacht is **clear astern** of another when her hull and equipment in normal position are abaft an imaginary line projected abeam from the aftermost point of the other's hull and equipment in normal position. The other yacht is **clear ahead**. . . . "

BLACK is clear astern of WHITE. As far as the rules are concerned it does not matter whether she is overtaking or not.

" . . . The yachts **overlap** if neither is **clear astern;** or if, although one is **clear astern,** an intervening yacht **overlaps** both of them . . . **"**

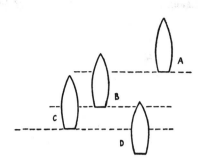

A and C are overlapped since an intervening yacht, B, overlaps both of them. (A and B are overlapped. B and C and D are overlapped.)

" . . . The terms **clear astern, clear ahead** and **overlap** apply to yachts on opposite **tacks** only when they are subject to rule 42—Rounding or Passing Marks and Obstructions. **"** (Page 55.)

Note rule 38.2—**Overlap Limitations:** "For the purpose of this rule" **(Right-of-Way Yacht Luffing after Starting):** "an **overlap** does not exist unless the yachts are clearly within two overall lengths of the longer yacht; and an **overlap** which exists between two yachts when the leading yacht **starts,** or when one or both of them completes a **tack** or **jibe,** shall be regarded as a new **overlap** beginning at that time."

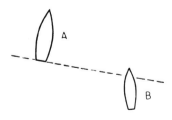

B overlaps A. She is not clear astern and is *within two of A's overall lengths.* B is considered as overlapping A, even though she is sailing a different course.

" Proper course*—A **proper course** is any course which a yacht might sail after the starting signal, in the absence of the other yacht or yachts affected, to **finish** as quickly as possible. The course sailed before **luffing** or **bearing away** is presumably, but not necessarily, that yacht's **proper course**. There is no **proper course** before the starting signal.

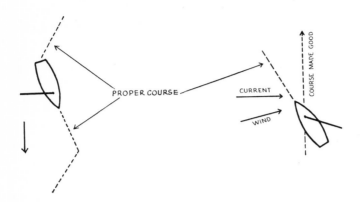

" Mark—A **mark** is any object specified in the sailing instructions which a yacht must round or pass on a required side.

Every ordinary part of a **mark** ranks as part of it, including a flag, flagpole, boom or hoisted boat, but excluding ground tackle and any object either accidentally or temporarily attached to the **mark. "**

" Obstruction—An **obstruction** is any object, including craft under way, large enough to require a yacht, if not less than one overall length away from it, to make a substantial alteration of course to pass on one side or the other, or any object which can be passed on one side only, including a buoy when the yacht in question cannot safely pass between it and the shoal or object which it marks. **"**

---

* In a decision of the Appeals Committee of the N.A.R.U. (No. 6) they state that "when there is doubt that a yacht is sailing above her proper course, she should be given the benefit of the doubt."

After rounding a mark, the proper course to the next mark must be taken "with reasonable promptness"—Appeal No. 12.

† Appeal No. 3 states: "A floating log or buoy that supports a mooring chain or rope to which a mark is attached is part of the 'ground tackle' of a mark and not part of the mark (Rule 52.2). Consequently there is no penalty for touching such a log or buoy, or any line or chain leading from it to the mark or to the submerged mooring."

Appeal No. 59 states: "If, however, fouling its ground tackle causes the mark to be drawn against the yacht, the mark has been touched and the yacht involved must, in accordance with Rule 52.1, retire immediately, or protest...etc."

This means that another yacht racing which has the right-of-way is an obstruction. Also, almost anything that would cause "a substantial alteration of course" would rank as one. Any normal size Committee Boat would not only be a mark of the course but an obstruction.

Naturally, the smaller the yacht, the smaller the object which could rank as an obstruction, but lobster-pot buoys or small mooring buoys would not be obstructions.

" **Cancellation**—A **cancelled** race is one which the Race Committee decides will not be sailed thereafter.

" **Postponement**—A **postponed** race is one which is not started at its scheduled time and which can be sailed at any time the Race Committee may decide.

" **Abandonment**—An **abandoned** race is one which the Race Committee declares void at any time after the starting signal, and which can be resailed at its discretion. "

SAILING RULES WHEN YACHTS MEET: N.A.Y.R.U. Rules, Part IV

" **Helmsman's Rights and Obligations Concerning Right of Way.** *The rules of Part IV apply only between yachts which either are intending to* race *or are* racing *in the same or different races, and, except when rule 3.2(b)(ii) applies, replace the International Regulations for Preventing Collisions at Sea or Government Right-of-Way Rules applicable to the area concerned, from the time a yacht intending to* race *begins to sail about in the vicinity of the starting line until she has either* finished *or retired and has left the vicinity of the course.*

" SECTION A—RULES WHICH ALWAYS APPLY

" 31—**Disqualification:**
1. A yacht may be disqualified or otherwise penalized for infringing a rule of Part IV only when the infringement occurs while she is **racing,** whether or not a collision results.
2. A yacht may be disqualified before or after she is **racing** for seriously hindering a yacht which is **racing,** or for infringing the sailing instructions.

" 32—**Avoiding Collisions:** A right-of-way yacht which fails to make a reasonable attempt to avoid a collision resulting in serious damage may be disqualified as well as the other yacht. "

Read new rule 67.

" 33—**Retiring from Race:** A yacht which realizes she has infringed a racing rule or a sailing instruction is under an obligation to retire promptly; but, when she persists in **racing,** other yachts shall continue to accord her such rights as she may have under the rules of Part IV. "

Left: WHITE is about to ram BLACK *amidships* or *farther aft.* Right: Both yachts should *bear off,* bows going in opposite directions.

WHITE is a starboard tack right-of-way yacht. Even so she shall try to avoid a collision.

Left: WHITE is about to ram BLACK *forward* of *amidships*. Right: Both yachts should *luff,* bows going in the same direction.

If WHITE fails to make a reasonable attempt to avoid a collision which results in serious damage, she may be disqualified as well as BLACK.

WHITE, port tack, is bearing off to go to leeward of BLACK, starboard tack right-of-way yacht. BLACK has begun to alter course in such a way as to prevent WHITE from keeping clear. If a collision occurs, BLACK can be disqualified. Even if there is no collision, she can be disqualified, if she "obstructs" her.

" 34—Right-of-Way Yacht Altering Course: When one yacht is required to keep clear of another, the right-of-way yacht shall not so alter course as to prevent the other yacht from keeping clear; so as to increase any alteration of course required of the other yacht in order to keep clear; or so as to obstruct her while she is keeping clear, except:
(a) to the extent permitted by rule 38.1, Right-of-Way Yacht Luffing after Starting, and
(b) when assuming a **proper course** to **start**, unless subject to the second part of rule 44.1 (b), Yachts Returning to Start. "

" 35—Hailing: 1. Except when **luffing** under rule 38.1, Luffing after Starting, a right-of-way yacht which does not hail before or when making an alteration of course which may not be forseen by the other yacht, may be disqualified as well as the yacht required to keep clear when a collision resulting in serious damage occurs.
2. A yacht which hails when claiming the establishment or termination of an **overlap** or insufficiency of room at a **mark** or **obstruction** thereby helps to support her claim for the purpose of rule 42, Rounding or Passing Marks and Obstructions. "

BLACK, port tack, must keep out of the way of WHITE, starboard tack. If WHITE has to alter course to avoid collision, BLACK may be disqualified.

If BLACK had been far enough ahead so as just to clear WHITE's bow, WHITE would not be allowed to luff to prevent her.

" SECTION B—OPPOSITE TACK RULE

" 36—Fundamental Rule: A **port-tack** yacht shall keep clear of a **starboard-tack** yacht.* **"**

---

* The decision in Appeal No. 32 states: "We hold that when there is reasonable doubt as to the ability of a port-tack yacht to cross ahead of a starboard-tack yacht, (1) the starboard-tack yacht is entitled to bear away and protest, and (2) the burden of proof rests on the port-tack yacht to prove that she would have cleared the starboard-tack yacht."

Rule 36 has two exceptions: Rule 42.1(a) **Rounding or Passing Marks and Obstructions . . . When Overlapped.** This states that when yachts either on the same tack or, after starting and clearing the starting line, on opposite tacks, are about to round or pass a mark on the same required side, with the exception of a starting mark surrounded by navigable water, or an obstruction on the same side: —An outside yacht* shall give each yacht overlapping her on the inside, room to round or pass it, except as provided in rules 42.1 (a)(iii), and (iv) and 42.3.

Also rule 44.1(a) **Yachts Returning to Start.** According to this rule a premature starter when returning to start, or a yacht working into position from the wrong side of the starting line or its extensions, when the starting signal is made, shall keep clear of all yachts which are starting, or have started, correctly, until she is wholly on the right side of the starting line or its extensions. Even a starboard-tack yacht must keep clear of a port-tack yacht which has started properly.

This Opposite Tack Rule applies *whether yachts are close-hauled or sailing free.* This means that a port-tack yacht close-hauled (for example, beating up to a windward mark) has to give way to a starboard-tack yacht sailing free.

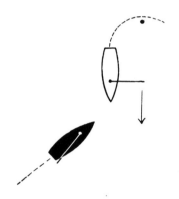

* Even a starboard-tack yacht.

" 37—Fundamental Rules:
  1. A **windward yacht** shall keep clear of a leeward yacht. "

According to definition, WHITE is a leeward yacht. BLACK must keep clear.

Even with yachts in this position, this rule applies. B must keep clear, since both yachts are on the same tack and neither is clear astern of the other. (See definition of "clear astern.")

" 2. A yacht **clear astern** shall keep clear of a yacht **clear ahead**. "

BLACK is clear astern and is overtaking WHITE. She must keep clear.

" 3. A yacht which establishes an **overlap** to **leeward** from **clear astern** shall allow the **windward yacht** ample room and opportunity to keep clear, and during the existence of that **overlap** the **leeward yacht** shall not sail above her **proper course**. "

See luffing limitations in rule 38.1, **"Right-of-Way Yacht Luffing after Starting,"** and rule 40, **"Right-of-Way Yacht Luffing before Starting."*** Rule 40 is new, and contains important changes.

* The overtaking yacht's obligation, when establishing an overlap to leeward, to allow the windward yacht ample room and opportunity to fulfill her newly acquired obligation to keep clear, cannot, except in a most exceptional case, be construed *"as a continuing one."* Appeal No. 36.

1. **Luffing Rights and Limitations.** After she has **started** and cleared the starting line, a yacht **clear ahead** or a leeward yacht may **luff** as she pleases . . . "

In the left-hand picture WHITE may luff BLACK "as she pleases," which means *head to wind if she pleases.** If the yachts are sailing dead before the wind, this could mean a luff of 180°.

Rule 38.1 continues ". . . EXCEPT THAT:

" A leeward yacht shall not sail above her **proper course** while an **overlap** exists if, at any time during its existence, the helmsman of the **windward yacht** (when sighting abeam from his normal station and sailing no higher than the **leeward yacht**) has been abreast or forward of the mainmast of the **leeward yacht.** "

In the right-hand picture, BLACK's helmsman has not yet come abreast of WHITE's main-mast. WHITE may luff as she pleases.

B has been luffing A, but A has gained on B to the point where A's helmsman is forward of B's mast. B may not sail above her proper course.

* The italicized words are those used in Appeal No. 42.

" 2. Overlap Limitations. For the purpose of this rule: An **overlap** does not exist unless the yachts are clearly within two overall lengths of the longer yacht; . . .

. . . and an **overlap** which exists between two yachts when the leading yacht **starts,** or when one or both of them completes a **tack** or **jibe,** shall be regarded as a new **overlap** beginning at that time. **"**

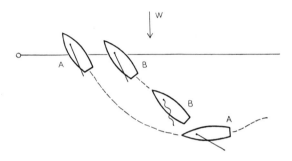

B having "loafed" at the line, was overtaken to leeward by A. A can now luff B, since their overlap began anew when they started.

A and B have just completed tacking. The overlap, for the purpose of rule 38.2, is regarded as beginning at the completion of the tack. A can luff B.

A and B are on opposite tacks in position No. 1. A has overtaken B. In position No. 2, A has jibed and can luff B, since A's mast is forward of B's helmsman and the overlap is considered as beginning when A has completed her jibe.

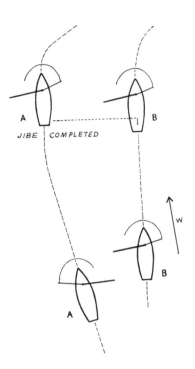

A   B

JIBE COMPLETED

W

B

A

" 3. **Hailing to Stop or Prevent a Luff.** When there is doubt, the **leeward yacht** may assume that she has the right to luff unless the helmsman of the **windward yacht** has hailed "Mast Abeam," or words to that effect. The leeward yacht shall be governed by such hail, and, if she deems it improper, her only remedy is to protest. "

Appeal No. 78 states: "The hailing provisions in Rule 38.3 were included in the "luffing rule" to reduce arguments and protests and they should be so interpreted. The helmsman of a windward yacht who fails to protect his rights by hailing in proper time is entitled to little consideration."

" It is easy for him to see when he attains the 'Mast Abeam' position. On the other hand, the helmsman of the leeward yacht is, as a rule, in no position to determine 'Mast Abeam.' Hence, he must rely on, and be governed by, a hail to know when he has lost his luffing rights. "

" A hail should, as a rule, be unnecessary when the leeward yacht established her overlap from clear astern. But when an overlap results from convergence, or the completion of a tack or jibe, we would hold the leeward yacht blameless if the helmsman of the windward yacht:

(*a*) that has attained the 'Mast Abeam' position fails to hail either before the leeward yacht begins to luff or the instant she begins to luff...

(*b*) that attains the 'Mast Abeam' position during a luff, fails to hail in time to enable the leeward yacht to bear away before contact. "

" 4. **Curtailing a Luff.** The **windward yacht** shall not cause a **luff** to be curtailed because of her proximity to the **leeward yacht** unless an **obstruction**, a third yacht or other object restricts her ability to respond.

" 5. **Luffing Two or More Yachts.** A yacht shall not luff unless she has the right to luff all yachts which would be affected by her **luff,** in which case they shall all respond even if an intervening yacht or yachts would not otherwise have the right to luff. "

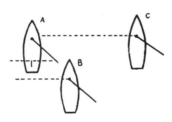

C has the right to luff windward yachts A and B. Although B would not other-wise have the right to luff A, B must respond to C's luff, and A must respond to B's luff. If B is overtaking A and C, she is thus given more protection than formerly in an effort to intervene.

Note also rule 42.1 (a)(iv): "An outside **leeward yacht** with luffing rights may take an inside yacht to windward of a **mark** provided that she hails to that effect and begins to **luff** before she is within two of her overall lengths of the **mark** and provided that she also passes to windward of it."

Appeal No. 20 states that a leeward yacht which has legally luffed a windward yacht may bear away suddenly, and that a windward yacht in responding to the luff is obliged to keep far enough away to give the leeward yacht "room to bear away both suddenly and rapidly."

On hailing, see Rules 35, 38.3, 43.1 and 43.2.

" 39—Sailing Below a Proper Course: A yacht which is on a free leg of the course shall not sail below her **proper course** when she is clearly within three of her overall lengths of either a **leeward yacht** or a yacht **clear astern** which is steering a course to pass to **leeward**. "

In picture No. 1, BLACK is within three of her overall lengths of WHITE, the leeward yacht. BLACK must not sail below her proper course.

In picture No. 2, BLACK is within three of her overall lengths of WHITE, who is steering a course to pass to leeward. BLACK must not sail below her proper course.

Note that this rule applies only to yachts on a *free* leg of the course. On a windward leg, the yacht to weather may bear off on a yacht in the act of passing her to leeward. She must, of course, obey the rule that a windward yacht shall keep clear of a leeward yacht.

" 40—Right-of-Way Yacht Luffing before Starting: Before a yacht has **started** and cleared the starting line, any **luff** on her part which causes another yacht to have to alter course to avoid a collision shall be carried out slowly and in such a way so as to give the **windward yacht** room and opportunity to keep clear, . . . **"**

WHITE must luff *slowly,* and in such a way as to give BLACK "room and opportunity to keep clear."

" . . . but the **leeward yacht** shall not so luff above a **close-hauled** course, unless the helmsman of the **windward yacht** (sighting abeam from his normal station) is abaft the mainmast of the **leeward yacht.** Rules 38.3, Hailing to Stop or Prevent a Luff; 38.4, Curtailing a Luff; and 38.5, Luffing Two or more Yachts, also apply. **"**

With new rule 40, if WHITE were aft of mast abeam she may not luff above a close-hauled course **after** the starting signal as well as before it.

41—Tacking or Jibing:
1. A yacht which is either **tacking** or **jibing** shall keep clear of a yacht **on a tack.**

BLACK has tacked too close to WHITE. WHITE has had to alter course to avoid a collision. Black should be disqualified. See following page.

" 2. A yacht shall neither **tack** nor **jibe** into a position which will give her right of way unless she does so far enough from a yacht **on a tack** to enable this yacht to keep clear without having to begin to alter her course until after the **tack** or **jibe** has been completed.

3. A yacht which **tacks** or **jibes** has the onus of satisfying the Race Committee that she completed her **tack** or **jibe** in accordance with rule 41.2. "

In the above picture, BLACK has gone over onto the starboard tack, which should give her the right-of-way, but she has tacked too close. WHITE need not begin to alter her course to keep clear until BLACK has *completed* her tack. BLACK should be disqualified because WHITE cannot keep clear.

Note rule 35, Hailing.

In the above picture, BLACK has tacked around the mark into a position that should subsequently give her right-of-way, but she has just borne away to a close-hauled course and WHITE cannot keep clear. BLACK should be disqualified. See following page.

" 4. When two yachts are both **tacking** or both **jibing** at the same time, the one on the other's **port** side shall keep clear. "

Both BLACK and WHITE are tacking. BLACK is on WHITE'S port side and must keep clear.

" *When a rule of this section applies, to the extent to which it explicitly provides rights and obligations, it overrides any conflicting rule of Part IV which precedes it, except the rules of Section A—Rules Which Always Apply.*

" 42—Rounding or Passing Marks and Obstructions: 1. Fundamental Rules Regarding Room. When yachts either on the same **tack** or, after **starting** and clearing the starting line, on opposite **tacks**, are about to round or pass a **mark** on the same required side, with the exception of a starting **mark** surrounded by navigable water, or an **obstruction** on the same side:

(*a*) When **Overlapped:**

    (i) An outside yacht shall give each yacht **overlapping** her on the inside, room to round or pass the **mark** or **obstruction**, except as provided in rules 42.1 (a)(iii), and (iv) and 42.3. Room includes room for an **overlapping** yacht to **tack** or **jibe** when either is an integral part of the rounding or passing manoeuvre. **"**

In the left-hand picture BLACK has not given WHITE room to tack around the mark. Note that in the right-hand picture, even though BLACK is on the starboard tack, she must still give·WHITE (port tack) room since both are about to round or pass* a mark on the required side. See following pages.

* Remember that it takes more room for a yacht to **"round"** a mark than to **"pass"** it, due to the swing of her stern. When a number of yachts are rounding a mark together, this extra room adds up, and is often underestimated by the outside yacht. In Appeal No. 64 an outside yacht was disqualified because the inside yacht had to let her spinnaker pole go forward to the headstay, and trim in her main boom, in order to avoid a collision.

" (ii) When an inside yacht of two or more **overlapped** yachts either on opposite **tacks,** or on the same **tack** without **luffing** rights, will have to **jibe** in order most directly to assume a **proper course** to the next **mark,** she shall **jibe** at the first reasonable opportunity. "

This provision does not grant permission to an inside starboard-tack yacht to carry her opponent past the mark. She must jibe "at the first reasonable opportunity."

" (iii) When two yachts on opposite **tacks** are on a beat or when one of them will have to **tack** either to round the **mark** or to avoid the **obstruction,** as between each other, rule 42.1 (a) (i) shall not apply and they are subject to rules 36, Opposite Tack Fundamental Rule, and 41, Tacking or Jibing.

(iv) An outside **leeward yacht** with luffing rights may take an inside yacht to windward of a **mark** provided that she hails to that effect and begins to **luff** before she is within two of her overall lengths of the **mark** and provided that she also passes to windward of it.

" 42 (b) **When Clear Astern and Clear Ahead**

(i) A yacht **clear astern** shall keep clear in anticipation of and during the rounding or passing maneuver when the yacht **clear ahead** remains on the same **tack** or **jibes.**

WHITE is clear ahead and will harden up and remain on the same tack. BLACK "shall keep clear."

" (ii) A yacht **clear ahead** which **tacks** to round a **mark** is subject to rule 41, Tacking or Jibing, but a yacht **clear astern** shall not **luff** above **close-hauled** so as to prevent the yacht **clear ahead** from **tacking.** "

" 42.2—Restrictions on Establishing and Maintaining an Overlap

(*a*) A yacht **clear astern** shall not establish an inside **overlap** and be entitled to room under rule 42.1 (a) when the yacht **clear ahead**:—

    (i) is within two of her overall lengths of the **mark** or **obstruction**, except as provided in rules 42.2(b) and 42.2(c).

    (ii) is unable to give the required room. **"**

BLACK established her inside overlap *after* WHITE was within two of her overall lengths of the mark. BLACK should be disqualified.

" 42.2(b) The two-lengths determinative above shall not apply to yachts, of which one has completed a tack within two overall lengths of a mark or an obstruction. **"**

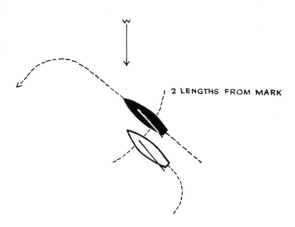

This rule gives WHITE the right to ask for room to pass on the required side of the mark, after she has completed her tack establishing an overlap on BLACK, *inside* the two-lengths-from-the-mark area.

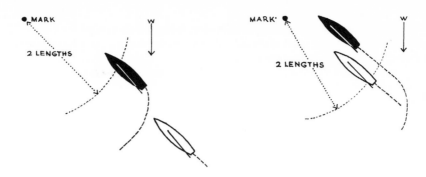

Left: BLACK has crossed in front of WHITE, and tacked to round the mark . . .
Right: WHITE has gained an overlap inside the 2-length limit (due to BLACK's slowing down while tacking). WHITE can now claim room.

"(*c*) A yacht **clear astern** may establish an **overlap** between the yacht **clear ahead** and a continuing **obstruction** such as a shoal or the shore, only when there is room for her to do so in safety.

(*d*) (i) A yacht **clear ahead** shall be under no obligation to give room to a yacht **clear astern** before an **overlap** is established.

(ii) A yacht which claims an inside **overlap** has the onus of satisfying the race committee that the **overlap** was established in proper time.

(*e*) (i) When an outside yacht is **overlapped** at the time she comes within two of her overall lengths of a **mark**, or an **obstruction**, she shall continue to be bound by rule 42.1(a)(i) to give room as required even though the **overlap** may thereafter be broken.

(ii) An outside yacht which claims to have broken an **overlap** has the onus of satisfying the race committee that she became **clear ahead** when she was more than two of her overall lengths from the **mark** or an **obstruction**.

(Anti-barging rule)

3. At a Starting Mark Surrounded by Navigable Water... (over)

"   When approaching the starting line to **start**, a **leeward yacht** shall be under no obligation to give any **windward yacht** room to pass to leeward of a starting **mark** surrounded by navigable water; . . . "

WHITE can hold her course and BLACK will be forced to pass on the wrong side of the mark.

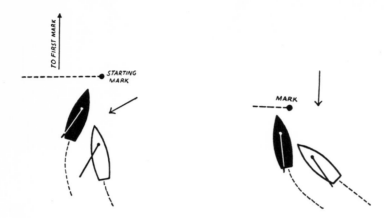

"   . . . But, after the starting signal, a **leeward yacht** shall not deprive a **windward yacht** of room at such a **mark** by sailing either above the first **mark** or above **close-hauled.** "

In the left diagram, the starting signal has gone. BLACK has headed above first mark and should be disqualified. Note that "first mark" means the first turning mark after the start.

    In the right diagram, the starting signal has gone. BLACK has luffed above close-hauled and should be disqualified.

    The diagram below represents a typical windward start. The starting signal has just been made. A (before the starting signal) has luffed B and B has luffed C. The dotted line indicates the close-hauled course to the starting mark.

    C, if she continues overlapped on B, is not entitled to room at the mark. D can make it ahead of B and can shut out E, since D is not sailing higher than close-hauled.

" 43—Close-Hauled, Hailing for Room to Tack at Obstructions

" 1. Hailing. When two **close-hauled** yachts are on the same **tack** and safe pilotage requires the yacht **clear ahead** or the **leeward yacht** to make a substantial alteration of course to clear an **obstruction,** and if she intends to **tack,** but cannot **tack** without colliding with the other yacht, she shall hail the other yacht for room to **tack** and clear the other yacht, but she shall not hail and tack simultaneously. **"**

Note that to do this:
1. Both yachts must be *close-hauled.*
2. Both yachts must be *on the same tack.*
3. Both yachts must be *approaching an obstruction.*
4. WHITE must have to *clear the obstruction.*
5. WHITE must have to make a *substantial alteration of course* to clear it.
6. WHITE must be *unable to tack without colliding* with BLACK.
7. *"Safe pilotage"* must require WHITE to take such action.

   Note that under the above rule (43.1), the situation illustrated below requires A to tack, even though the obstruction* (C) is not a mark. (See rule 43.3(*a*).)

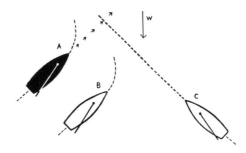

C is a right-of-way yacht (starboard tack). B has hailed A for room to tack. *Even though A can cross C's bow,* she must respond to B's hail.

* See definition of Obstruction . . . "any object, including craft under way . . ."

" 2. Responding. The hailed yacht at the earliest possible moment after the hail shall either:—

(*a*) **tack,** in which case, the hailing yacht shall begin to **tack** either:—

    (i) before the hailed yacht has completed her **tack,** or

    (ii) if she cannot then **tack** without colliding with the hailed yacht, immediately she is able to **tack** and clear her, or

(*b*) reply "You **tack,**" or words to that effect, if in her opinion she can keep clear without **tacking** or after postponing her **tack.** In this case:—

    (i) the hailing yacht shall immediately **tack** and

    (ii) the hailed yacht shall keep clear.

    (iii) The onus shall lie on the hailed yacht which replied "You **tack**" to satisfy the Race Committee that she kept clear. **"**

BLACK has replied, "You tack" to WHITE's hail. WHITE has tacked; BLACK has kept clear.

" 43.3—Limitation on Right to Room when the Obstruction is a Mark.

(*a*) When the hailed yacht can fetch an **obstruction** which is also a **mark,** the hailing yacht shall not be entitled to room to **tack** and clear the other yacht and the hailed yacht shall immediately so inform the hailing yacht.

(*b*) If, thereafter, the hailing yacht again hails for room to **tack** and clear the other yacht she shall, after receiving it, retire immediately.

(c) If, after having refused to respond to a hail under rule 43.3(a), the hailed yacht fails to fetch, she shall retire immediately. **"**

BLACK may not hail for room to tack, since WHITE can fetch the obstruction, which in this case is a mark (the Committee Boat). If BLACK cannot bear off to avoid the Committee Boat and must tack, she shall hail again, and *retire immediately.*

"44—Yachts Returning to Start

1. (*a*) A premature starter when returning to **start,** or a yacht working into position from the wrong side of the starting line or its extensions, when the starting signal is made, shall keep clear of all yachts which are **starting,** or have **started,** correctly, until she is wholly on the right side of the starting line or its extensions.

(*b*) Thereafter, she shall be accorded the rights under the rules of Part IV of a yacht which is **starting** correctly; but if she thereby acquires right of way over another yacht which is **starting** correctly, she shall allow that yacht ample room and opportunity to keep clear.

2. A premature starter while continuing to sail the course and until it is obvious that she is returning to **start,** shall be accorded the rights under the rules of Part IV of a yacht which has **started.** "

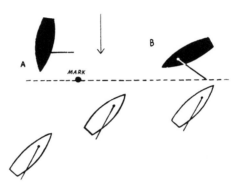

The starting signal has just been made. B has started prematurely. A is working into position from the wrong side of the extension of the starting line. A and B, even though on the starboard tack, must keep clear of all yachts starting properly. (A and B, in relation to each other, must abide by all applicable rules.)

"45—Yachts Re-rounding after Touching a Mark

1. A yacht which has touched a **mark** and is about to exonerate herself in accordance with rule 52.2, Touching a Mark, shall keep clear of all other yachts which are about to round or pass it or have rounded or passed it correctly, until she has rounded it completely and has cleared it and is on a **proper course** to the next **mark.**

2. A yacht which has touched a **mark,** while continuing to sail the course and until it is obvious that she is returning to round it completely in accordance with rule 52.2, Touching a Mark, shall be accorded rights under the rules of Part IV.

" SECTION F—WHEN NOT UNDER WAY

"46—Anchored, Aground or Capsized

1. A yacht under way shall keep clear of another yacht **racing** which is anchored, aground or capsized. Of two anchored yachts, the one which anchored later shall keep clear, except that a yacht which is dragging shall keep clear of one which is not. "

A, a yacht which is dragging, must keep clear of B, even though B anchored after A.

" 2. A yacht anchored or aground shall indicate the fact to any yacht which may be in danger of fouling her. Unless the size of the yachts or the weather conditions make some other signal necessary, a hail is sufficient indication.
3. A yacht shall not be penalized for fouling a yacht in distress which she is attempting to assist nor a yacht which goes aground or capsizes immediately ahead of her. "

OTHER SAILING RULES:
N.A.Y.R.U. Rules, Part V

" OBLIGATIONS OF HELMSMAN AND CREW IN HANDLING A YACHT

" Except for rule 49, a yacht is subject to the rules of Part V only while she is **racing.**

" 49—Fair Sailing: A yacht shall attempt to win a race only by fair sailing, superior speed and skill, and, except in team races, by individual effort. However, a yacht may be disqualified under this rule only in the case of a clear-cut violation of the above principles and only if no other rule applies. **"**

This provision prohibits two or more yachts in a *fleet* race from collaborating to hinder another yacht.

" 51—Sailing the Course "

" 1.(*c*) Unless otherwise prescribed in the sailing instructions, when after a general recall, any part of a yacht's hull, crew or equipment is on the course side of the starting line or its extentions during the minute before her starting signal, she shall thereafter return to the pre-start side of the line across one of its extentions and **start. "**

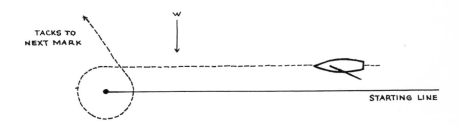

Now it is not enough simply to go behind the starting line and start again. You must go to the end of the starting line and circle the mark or the committee boat.

" 1.(*d*) Failure of a yacht to see or hear her recall notification shall not relieve her of her obligation to **start** correctly. "

Read new rule 51.3 on limit marks.

" **52—Touching a Mark**
    1. A yacht which either:—
      (*a*) touches:—
          (i) a starting **mark** before **starting;**
          (ii) a **mark** which begins, bounds or ends the leg of the course **on which she** is sailing; or
          (iii) a finishing **mark** after **finishing,** or
      (*b*) causes a **mark** or **mark** vessel to shift to avoid being touched, shall retire immediately, unless either:
          (i) she alleges that she was wrongfully compelled by another yacht to touch it or cause it to shift, in which case she shall protest or
          (ii) she exonerates herself in accordance with rule 52.2.
    2.(*a*) Unless otherwise prescribed in the sailing instructions, a yacht which touches a **mark** surrounded by navigable water may exonerate herself by completing one entire rounding of the **mark,** leaving it on the required side, and thereafter she shall re-round or re-pass it, without touching it, as required to sail the course in accordance with rule 51, Sailing the Course, and the sailing instructions.
      (*b*) When a yacht touches:
          (i) a starting **mark,** she shall carry out the rounding after she has **started;** or
          (ii) a finishing **mark,** she shall carry out the rounding, and she shall not rank as having finished until she has completed the rounding and again crosses the finishing line in accordance with the definition of **finishing.** "

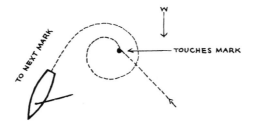

Now a yacht does not have to "retire immediately." By following the above rule, she can continue to race.

" 52.2 For the purposes of rule 52.1: Every ordinary part of a **mark** ranks as part of it, including a flag, flagpole, boom or hoisted boat, but excluding ground tackle and any object either accidentally or temporarily attached to it. "
Appeal No. 59 states that if fouling a mark's ground tackle causes the mark to be drawn against the yacht, "the mark has been touched and the yacht involved must, in accordance with Rule 52.1, retire immediately, or protest . . . etc."

" **54—Setting and Sheeting Sails**
    1. **Changing Sails.** While changing headsails and spinnakers a replacing sail may be fully set and trimmed before the sail it replaces is taken in, but only one mainsail and, except when changing, only one spinnaker shall be carried set. "

" 54.2 ... no sails shall be sheeted over or through outriggers.

Appeal No. 125 ... "the crew was pressing the jib sheet down and outboard of the hull of the yacht with her foot while the yacht was on a reach ... " Decision: "No part of the human body is an outrigger or fitting."

Appeal No. 148 "In very light air during a broad reaching leg of the course a crew member ... from his station aft of the mast supported the mid-section of the spinnaker with a paddle."
Decision: "Rules 54.2 and 54.3 deal with sheeting and setting headsails at points outside of a vertical line from the hull (or deck planking) of a yacht when upright. "Since the paddle neither extended beyond the verticles, nor exerted outward pressure on a sheet, the manner in which it was used did not contravene Rules 54.2 or 54.3."

" 60—Means of Propulsion

A yacht shall be propelled only by the natural action of the wind on the sails, spars and hull, and water on the hull, and shall not pump, "ooch" or rock, as described in Appendix 2, nor check way by abnormal means, except for the purpose of rule 58, Rendering Assistance, or of recovering a man who has accidentally fallen overboard. An oar, paddle or other object may be used in emergency for steering. An anchor may be sent out in a boat only as permitted by rule 64, Aground or Foul of an Obstruction. "

Appeal No. 56 adds considerably to the interpretation of rule 60. It states:
" In view of the fact found by the Race Committee that EASTWIND did not resort to "sculling" and that her skipper, while moving his tiller to starboard several times before reaching mark "B" and to port several times after reaching the mark, did not bring it *beyond amidships*, the purpose and result of his action being only to alter the course of his yacht and not to give her headway, we are of the opinion that his action did not constitute an infraction of Rule 60. "

" 62—Manual Power

A yacht shall use manual power only, except that a power winch or windlass may be used in weighing anchor or in getting clear after running aground or fouling any object, and a power bilge pump may be used in an auxiliary yacht. "

" 66—Increasing Stability

Unless otherwise prescribed by her class rules or in the sailing instructions, a yacht shall not use any device, such as a trapeze or plank, to project outboard the weight of any of the crew, nor, when a yacht is equipped with lifelines, shall any member of the crew station any part of his torso outside them, other than temporarily. "

Note that this is now a Rule, not just a class rule or sailing instruction.

See "Pumping" Sails, "Ooching" and "Rocking," page 69.

PROTESTS, DISQUALIFICATIONS AND APPEALS:
N.A.Y.R.U. Rules, Part VI

" 67—Contact between Yachts Racing

1. When there is contact between the hull, spars, standing rigging or crew of two yachts while racing, both shall be disqualified, unless one of them retires in acknowledgement of an infringement of the rules, or one or both of them acts in accordance with rule 68.3, Protests.

2. A third yacht which witnesses an apparent collision between two yachts and, after finishing or retiring, discovers that neither of them has observed rule 67.1, is relieved by rule 68.3 (b) from the requirement of showing a protest flag and may lodge a protest against them.

3. The Race Committee may waive this rule when it is satisfied that minor contact was unavoidable. **"**

This new rule does not apply when contact consists only of a spinnaker or spinnaker sheet.

" 68—Protests

1. A yacht can protest against any other yacht . . .

Appeal No. 101 states: " 'Can' is permissive, not obligatory."

3. (*a*) A protest for an infringement of the rules or sailing instructions occurring during a race shall be signified by showing a flag (International Code flag "B" is always acceptable, irrespective of any other provisions in the sailing instructions) conspicuously in the rigging of the protesting yacht at the first reasonable opportunity and keeping it flying until she has **finished** or retired, or if the first reasonable opportunity occurs after **finishing,** until acknowledged by the race committee . . .

Appeal No. 88 states: "We hold that for purposes of rule 68 'flag' should be broadly interpreted and may include makeshifts such as a handkerchief, provided the sailing instructions do not specify a particular flag. Accordingly, the prompt display of a red cellophane tell-tale met the local requirements for a 'red flag.' "

Appeal No. 105 finds that the protesting yacht had displayed a protest flag "at the first reasonable opportunity"; in this case, "after rounding the first mark located about two miles beyond the incident protested."

Continuing rule 68:

" . . . In the case of a yacht sailed single-handed, it will be sufficient if the flag (whether displayed in the rigging or not) is brought to the notice of the yacht protested against as soon as possible after the incident and to the race committee when the protesting yacht finishes. **"**

Note Rule 68.3(e) on action to be taken by protesting yacht.

THE
YACHT RACING RULES
INCLUDING
TEAM RACING RULES
OF THE
INTERNATIONAL YACHT
RACING UNION
AS ADOPTED BY THE
NORTH AMERICAN
YACHT RACING UNION
1973

(No changes contemplated until 1977)

North American Yacht Racing Union

37 West 44th Street   New York, N.Y. 10036

NOTE:
**In translating and interpreting these rules, it shall be understood that the word "shall"
is mandatory, and the words "can" and "may" are permissive.**

Right of way when not subject to the racing rules
The rules of Part IV do not apply in any way to a vessel which is neither intending to race
nor racing; such vessel shall be treated in accordance with the International Regulations for
Preventing Collisions at Sea or Government Right-of-Way Rules applicable in the area
concerned.
See Appendix 8.

1973 CHANGES
As in 1969, the 1973 rules include a good many small changes for consistency and better
understanding.

Rules 22.3, 67, 74.3 and Appendix 3 are new. So also, but of different application, are
Appendices 4 and 5.

Without implying that other changes need not be examined, attention is called to rules
32, 34, 35, 40, 42.1 (*a*) (ii), 52.2, 73.2(*b*), the team racing rules and Appendix 6.

For ready comparison most changes, even when only the number of the rule, are
indicated by a vertical line in the left margin.

FOREWORD

Effective May 1, 1973, the North American Yacht Racing Union has adopted as its official racing rules the racing rules, including the team racing rules, of the International Yacht Racing Union. No changes are contemplated until 1977.

The I.Y.R.U. rules permit certain changes and additions by national authorities. In order to assist North American yachtsmen when racing abroad and visiting yachtsmen when racing here, rules so changed or added have been identified by placing a star ($\star$) in the margin beside them.

Of the twenty-three rules listed in this paragraph the following eight rules have been changed by the N.A.Y.R.U. and have been starred ($\star$) except rule 72.4 which has been deleted. The I.Y.R.U. text of these rules is given in Appendix 7.

    8.1, 18, 24, 25.2, 28, 72.4, 77, 78.

The following fifteen rules have not been changed by the N.A.Y.R.U. other than to be printed without the phrase "unless otherwise prescribed (or if so prescribed) by the national authority" or words to that effect:

    1.4, 2(j), 3.1, 3.2(b) (xvi), 4.1, 4.2, 4.4(a), 10, 23, 24, 52.2, 54.2, 56; 57, 62.

All the above twenty-three rules should be checked for differences when sailing under the jurisdiction of another national authority.

A graduated penalty in Appendix 3 and a prescription to rule 68.4(a) in Appendix 6 have been added and starred ($\star$).

The following three starred ($\star$) rules have been added by the N.A.Y.R.U. on matters not covered by I.Y.R.U. rules:

    51.6, 53.2, 79.

North American yachtsmen will find the above information of significance to them only when racing under the jurisdiction of another national authority. For racing under the jurisdiction of the N.A.Y.R.U. the starred ($\star$) rules are to be treated like any other rules.

PART 1   DEFINITIONS

When a term defined in Part 1 is used in its defined sense it is printed in **bold** *type. All definitions and italicized notes rank as rules.*

    Racing—A yacht is **racing** from her preparatory signal until she has either **finished** and cleared the finishing line and finishing **marks** or retired, or until the race has been **cancelled, postponed** or **abandoned,** except that in match or team races, the sailing instructions may prescribe that a yacht is **racing** from any specified time before the preparatory signal.

    Starting—A yacht **starts** when, after fulfilling her penalty obligations, if any, under rule 51.1(c), Sailing the Course, and after her starting signal, any part of her hull, crew or equipment first crosses the starting line in the direction of the course to the first **mark.**

    Finishing—A yacht **finishes** when any part of her hull, or of her crew or equipment in normal position, crosses the finishing line from the direction of the course from the last **mark,** after fulfilling her penalty obligations, if any, under rule 52.2, Touching a Mark.

    Luffing—Altering course towards the wind until head to wind.

    Tacking—A yacht is **tacking** from the moment she is beyond head to wind until she has **borne away,** if beating to windward, to a **close-hauled** course; if not beating to windward, to the course on which her mainsail has filled.

    Bearing Away—Altering course away from the wind until a yacht begins to **jibe.**

    Jibing—A yacht begins to **jibe** at the moment when, with the wind aft, the foot of her mainsail crosses her centre line and completes the **jibe** when the mainsail has filled on the other **tack.**

On a Tack—A yacht is **on a tack** except when she is **tacking** or **jibing**. A Yacht is on the **tack** (**starboard** or **port**) corresponding to her **windward** side.

Close-hauled—A yacht is **close-hauled** when sailing by the wind as close as she can lie with advantage in working to windward.

Clear Astern and Clear Ahead; Overlap—A yacht is **clear astern** of another when her hull and equipment in normal position are abaft an imaginary line projected abeam from the aftermost point of the other's hull and equipment in normal position. The other yacht is **clear ahead**. The yachts **overlap** if neither is **clear astern**; or if, although one is **clear astern**, an intervening yacht **overlaps** both of them. The terms **clear astern**, **clear ahead** and **overlap** apply to yachts on opposite **tacks** only when they are subject to rule 42, Rounding or Passing Marks and Obstructions.

Leeward and Windward—The **leeward** side of a yacht is that on which she is, or, if **luffing** head to wind, was, carrying her mainsail. The opposite side is the **windward** side.

When neither of two yachts on the same **tack** is **clear astern**, the one on the **leeward** side of the other is the **leeward yacht**. The other is the **windward yacht**.

Proper course—A **proper course** is any course which a yacht might sail after the starting signal, in the absence of the other yacht or yachts affected, to **finish** as quickly as possible. The course sailed before **luffing** or **bearing away** is presumably, but not necessarily, that yacht's **proper course**. There is no **proper course** before the starting signal.

Mark—A **mark** is any object specified in the sailing instructions which a yacht must round or pass on a required side.

Every ordinary part of a **mark** ranks as part of it, including a flag, flagpole, boom or hoisted boat, but excluding ground tackle and any object either accidentally or temporarily attached to the **mark**.

Obstruction—An **obstruction** is any object, including craft under way, large enough to require a yacht, if not less than one overall length away from it, to make a substantial alteration of course to pass on one side or the other, or any object which can be passed on one side only, including a buoy when the yacht in question cannot safely pass between it and the shoal or object which it marks.

Cancellation—A **cancelled** race is one which the race committee decides will not be sailed thereafter.

Postponement—A **postponed** race is one which is not started at its scheduled time and which can be sailed at any time the race committee may decide.

Abandonment—An **abandoned** race is one which the race committee declares void at any time after the starting signal, and which can be re-sailed at its discretion.

PART II   MANAGEMENT OF RACES

Authority and Duties of Race Committee
The rules of Part II deal with the duties and responsibilities of the race committee in conducting a race, the meaning of signals made by it and of other actions taken by it.

1—General Authority of Race Committee and Jury or Judges
1. All races shall be arranged, conducted and judged by a race committee under the direction of the sponsoring organization, except as may be provided under rule 1.2. The race committee may delegate the conduct of a race, the hearing and deciding of protests or any other of its responsibilities to one or more sub-committees which, if appointed, will hereinafter be included in the term "race committee" wherever it is used.

2. For a special regatta or series, the sponsoring organization may provide for a jury or judges to hear and decide protests and to have supervision over the conduct of the races, in which case the race committee shall be subject to the direction of the jury or judges to the extent provided by the sponsoring organization.

3. All yachts entered or **racing** shall be subject to the direction and control of the race committee, but it shall be the sole responsibility of each yacht to decide whether or not to **start** or to continue to **race**.

4. The race committee may reject any entry without stating the reason.

However, at all world and continental championships, no entry within established quotas shall be rejected without first obtaining the approval of the I.Y.R.U. or the duly authorized international class association.

5. The race committee shall be governed by these rules, by the prescriptions of its national authority, by the sailing instructions, by approved class rules (but it may refuse to recognize any class rule which conflicts with these rules) and, when applicable, by the international team racing rules, and shall decide all questions in accordance therewith.

2—Notice of Race
The notice of a race or regatta shall contain the following information:—

(*a*) That the race or races will be sailed under the rules of the I.Y.R.U., the prescriptions of the national authority and the rules of each class concerned.

(*b*) The date and place of the regatta and the time of the start of the first race and, if possible, succeeding races.

(*c*) The class or classes for which races will be given.

The notice shall also cover such of the following matters as may be appropriate:—

(*d*) Any special instructions, subject to rule 3.1, which may vary or add to these rules or class rules.

(*e*) Any restrictions or conditions regarding entries and numbers of starters or competitors.

(*f*) The address to which entries shall be sent, the date on which they close, the amount of entrance fees, if any, and any other entry requirements.

(*g*) Particulars and number of prizes.

(*h*) Time and place for receiving sailing instructions.

(*i*) Scoring system.

(*j*) That for the purpose of determining the result of a race which is one of a series of races in a competition, decisions of protests shall not be subject to appeal if it is essential to establish the results promptly.

3—The Sailing Instructions
1. **Status**—These rules shall be supplemented by written sailing instructions which shall rank as rules and may alter a rule by specific reference to it, but except in accordance with rule 3.2(b)(ii) they shall not alter Parts I and IV of these rules; provided however, that this restriction shall not preclude the right of developing and testing proposed rule changes in local regattas.

2. **Contents**—(*a*) The sailing instructions shall contain the following information:—

(i) That the race or races will be sailed under the rules of the I.Y.R.U., the prescriptions of the National Authority, the sailing instructions and the rules of each class concerned.

(ii) The course or courses to be sailed or a list of **marks** or courses from which the course or courses will be selected, describing all **marks** and stating the order in which and the side on which each is to be rounded or passed.

(iii) The course signals.

(iv) The classes to race and class signals, if any.

(v) Time of start for each class.

(vi) Starting line and starting area if used.

(vii) Finishing line and any special instructions for shortening the course or for **finishing** a shortened course. (Where possible it is good practice for the sailing instructions for **finishing** a shortened course not to differ from those laid down for **finishing** the full course.)

(viii) Time limit, if any, for **finishing**.

(ix) Scoring system, if not previously announced in writing, including the method, if any, for breaking ties.

(*b*) The sailing instructions shall also cover such of the following matters as may be appropriate:—

   (i) The date and place of the race or races.

  (ii) When the race is to continue after sunset, the time or place, if any, at which the International Regulations for Preventing Collisions at Sea, or Government Right-of-Way Rules, shall replace the corresponding rules of Part IV, and the night signals the committee boat will display.

 (iii) Any special instructions, subject to rule 3.1, which may vary or add to these rules, or class rules, and any special signals.

 (iv) Eligibility; entry; measurement certificate; declaration.

  (v) Any special instruction or signal, if any, regarding the carrying on board and wearing of personal buoyancy.

 (vi) Names, national letters and distinguishing numbers and ratings, if any, of the yachts entered.

 (vii) Any special instructions governing the methods of starting and recall.

(viii) Recall numbers or letters, if used, of the yachts entered.

 (ix) Time allowances.

  (x) Length of course or courses.

 (xi) Method by which competitors will be notified of any change of course.

 (xii) Information on tides and currents.

(xiii) Prizes.

(xiv) When rule 68.7, Alternative Penalties, if used, will apply.

 (xv) Any special time limit within which, and address at which, a written protest shall be lodged, and the prescribed fee, if any, which shall accompany it.

(xvi) Time and place at which protests will be heard.

(xvii) That for the purpose of determining the result of a race which is one of a series of races in a competition, decisions of protests shall not be subject to appeal if it is essential to establish the results promptly.

(xviii) Whether races **postponed** or **abandoned** for the day will be sailed later and, if so, when and where.

(xix) Disposition to be made of a yacht appearing at the start alone in her class.

 (xx) Time and place at which results of races will be posted.

3. **Distribution**—The sailing instructions shall be available to each yacht entitled to race.

4. **Changes**—The race committee may change the sailing instructions by notice, in writing if practicable, given to each yacht affected not later than the warning signal of her class.

5. **Oral Instructions**—Oral instructions shall not be given except in accordance with procedure specifically set out in the sailing instructions.

4—Signals

1. **International Code Flag Signals**—Unless otherwise prescribed in the sailing instructions the following International Code flags shall be used as indicated and when displayed alone they shall apply to all classes, and when displayed over a class signal they shall apply to the designated class only:

"AP" Answering Pennant—Postponement Signal.

   (*a*) Means:—

"All races not started are **postponed**.

The warning signal will be made one minute after this signal is lowered."

(One sound signal shall be made with the lowering of the "AP".)

   (*b*) Over one ball or shape, means:—

"The scheduled starting times of all races not started are **postponed** fifteen minutes."

(This postponement can be extended indefinitely by the addition of one ball or shape for every fifteen minutes).

(*c*) Over one of the numeral pennants 1 to 9, means:—
"All races not started are **postponed** one hour, two hours, etc."
(*d*) Over the letter "A", means:—
"All races not started are **postponed** to a later date."

"B"—Protest signal.
  When displayed by a yacht means:—
    "I intend to lodge a protest."

"L"—Means:—
    "Come within hail." or "Follow Me."

"M"—Mark Signal.
  When displayed on a buoy, vessel, or other object, means:—
    "Round or pass the object displaying this signal instead of the **mark** which it
    replaces."

"N"—Abandonment Signal.
  Means:—
    "All races are abandoned."

"N over X"—Abandonment and Re-Sail Signal.
  Means:—
    "All races are abandoned and will shortly be re-sailed. Watch for fresh **starting**
    signals."

"N over First Repeater"—Cancellation Signal.
  Means:—
    "All races are cancelled."

"P"—Preparatory Signal.
  Means:—
    "The class designated by the warning signal will start in 5 minutes exactly."

"R"—Reverse Course Signal.
  Alone, means:—
    "Sail the course prescribed in the sailing instructions in the reverse direction."
  When displayed over a course signal, means:—
    "Sail the designated course in the reverse direction."

"S"—Shorten Course Signal.
  (*a*) at or near the starting line, means:—
    "Sail the shortened course prescribed in the sailing instructions."
  (*b*) at or near the finishing line, means:—
  "**Finish** the race either:
      (i) at the prescribed finishing line at the end of the round still to be completed
      by the leading yacht" or
      (ii) "in any other manner prescribed in the sailing instructions under rule
      3.2(*a*)(vii)."
  (*c*) at or near a rounding **mark**, means:—
    "**Finish**" between the nearby **mark** and the committee boat."

"1st Repeater"—General Recall Signal.

Means:—

"The class is recalled for a fresh start as provided in sailing instructions."

2. Signaling the Course—The race committee shall either make the appropriate course signal or otherwise designate the course before or with the warning signal.

3. Changing the Course—The course for a class which has not **started** may be changed:—

(*a*) by displaying the appropriate **postponement** signal and indicating the new course before or with the warning signal to be displayed after the lowering of the **postponement** signal; or

(*b*) by displaying a course signal or by removing and substituting a course signal before or with the warning signal.

(Method (*a*) is preferable when a change of course involves either shifting the committee boat or other starting mark, or requires a change of sails which cannot reasonably be completed within the 5-minute period before the preparatory signal is made.)

4. Signals for Starting a Race

(*a*) Unless otherwise prescribed in the sailing instructions, the signals for starting a race shall be made at 5-minute intervals exactly, and shall be either:—

(i) *Warning Signal* — Class flag broken out or distinctive signal displayed.

Preparatory Signal — Code flag "P" broken out or distinctive signal displayed.

Starting Signal — Both warning and preparatory signals lowered.

In system (i) when classes are started:—

(a) at ten-minute intervals, the warning signal for each succeeding class shall be broken out or displayed at the starting signal of the preceding class, and

(b) at five-minute intervals, the preparatory signal for the first class to start shall be left flying or displayed until the last class has started. The warning signal for each succeeding class shall be broken out or displayed at the preparatory signal of the preceding class, or

(ii) *Warning signal* — White shape.

Preparatory Signal — Blue shape.

Starting Signal — Red shape.

first class to start

In system (ii) each signal shall be lowered 30 seconds before the hoisting of the next, and in starting yachts by classes, the starting signal for each class shall be the preparatory signal for the next.

(*b*) Although rule 4.4(*a*) specifies 5-minute intervals between signals, this shall not interfere with the power of a race committee to start a series of races at any intervals which it considers desirable.

(*c*) A warning signal shall not be made before its scheduled time, except with the consent of all yachts entitled to race.

(*d*) When a significant error is made in the timing of the interval between any of the signals for starting a race, the recommended procedure is to have a general recall, **abandonment** or **postponement** of the race whose start is directly affected by the error and a corresponding **postponement** of succeeding races. Unless otherwise prescribed in the sailing instructions a new warning signal shall be made. When the race is not recalled, **abandoned** or **postponed** after an error in the timing of the interval, each succeeding signal shall be made at the correct interval from the preceding signal.

5. Finishing Signals—Blue flag or shape. When displayed at the finish, means—"The committee boat is on station at the finishing line."

6. Other Signals—The sailing instructions shall designate any other special signals and shall explain their meaning.

7. Calling Attention to Signals—Whenever the race committee makes a signal, except "R" or "S" before the warning signal, it shall call attention to its action as follows:—

Three guns or other sound signals when displaying "N," "N over X," or "N over 1st Repeater."

Two guns or other sound signals when displaying the "1st Repeater," "AP," or "S."

One gun or other sound signal when making any other signal, including the lowering of "AP" when the length of the postponement is not signalled.

8. **Visual Signal to Govern**—Times shall be taken from the visual starting signals, and a failure or mistiming of a gun or other sound signal shall be disregarded.

5—Cancelling, Postponing or Abandoning a Race and Changing or Shortening Course

1. The race committee:—

(a) before the starting signal may shorten the course or **cancel** or **postpone** a race for any reason, and

(b) after the starting signal may shorten the course by finishing a race at any rounding **mark** or **cancel** or **abandon** a race because of foul weather endangering the yachts, or because of insufficient wind, or because a **mark** is missing or has shifted or for other reasons directly affecting safety or the fairness of the competition.

(c) after the starting signal may change the course at any rounding **mark** subject to proper notice being given to each yacht as prescribed in the sailing instructions.

2. After a **postponement** the ordinary starting signals prescribed in rule 4.4(a) shall be used, and the postponement signal, if a general one, shall be hauled down before the first warning or course signal is made.

3. The race committee shall notify all yachts concerned by signal or otherwise when and where a race **postponed** or **abandoned** will be sailed.

6—Starting and Finishing Lines

The starting and finishing lines shall be either:—

(a) A line between a **mark** and a mast or staff on the committee boat or station clearly identified in the sailing instructions;

(b) a line between two **marks;** or

(c) the extension of a line through two stationary posts, with or without a **mark** at or near its outer limit, inside which the yachts shall pass.

For types (a) and (c) of starting or finishing lines the sailing instructions may also prescribe that a **mark** will be laid at or near the inner end of the line, in which case yachts shall pass between it and the outer **mark**.

7—Start of a Race

1. **Starting Area**—The sailing instructions may define a starting area which may be bounded by buoys; if so, they shall not rank as **marks**.

2. **Timing the Start**—The start of a yacht shall be timed from her starting signal.

8—Recalls

☆ 1. Yachts' sail numbers shall be used as recall numbers except that the Race Committee may instead allot a suitable recall number or letter to each yacht in accordance with rule 3.2(b)(viii).

2. When, at her starting signal, any part of a yacht's hull, crew or equipment is on the course side of the starting line or its extensions, or she is subject to rule 51.1(c), Sailing the Course, the Race Committee shall:

(a) when each yacht has been allotted a recall number or letter, display her recall number or letter as soon as possible and make a suitable sound signal. As soon as the recalled yacht has wholly returned to the pre-start side of the line or its extensions, the Race Committee shall so inform her by removing her recall number or letter. This is the preferred procedure.

(b) When no recall number or letter has been allotted, make a sound signal and leave the class warning signal at "the dip" or display such other signal as may be prescribed in the sailing instructions, until she has wholly returned to the pre-start side of the line or its extensions, or for such shorter period as the Race Committee considers reasonable. The responsibility for returning shall rest with the yacht concerned.

(*c*) Follow such other procedure as may be prescribed in the sailing instructions.

3. (*a*) When there is either a number of unidentified premature starters, or an error in starting procedure, the Race Committee may make a general recall signal in accordance with rules 4.1, "First Repeater", and 4.7 Calling Attention to Signals. Unless otherwise prescribed in the sailing instructions, new warning and preparatory signals shall be made.

(*b*) Except as provided in rule 31.2, Disqualification, rule infringements before the preparatory signal for the new start shall be disregarded for the purpose of starting in the race to be re-started.

9—Marks
1. Mark Missing
(*a*) When any **mark** either is missing or has shifted, the race committee shall, if possible, replace it in its stated position, or substitute a new one with similar characteristics or a buoy or vessel displaying the letter "M" of the International Code—the **mark** signal.

(*b*) If it is impossible either to replace the **mark** or to substitute a new one in time for the yachts to round or pass it, the Race Committee may, at its discretion, act in accordance with rule 5.1, Cancelling, Postponing or Abandoning a Race and Changing or Shortening Course.

2. **Mark Unseen**—When races are sailed in fog or at night, dead reckoning alone should not necessarily be accepted as evidence that a **mark** has been rounded or passed.

10—Finishing Within a Time Limit
Unless otherwise prescribed in the sailing instructions, in races where there is a time limit, one yacht **finishing** within the prescribed limit shall make the race valid for all other yachts in that race.

11—Ties
When there is a tie at the finish of a race, either actual or on corrected times, the points for the place for which the yachts have tied and for the place immediately below shall be added together and divided equally. When two or more yachts tie for a trophy or prize in either a single race or a series, the yachts so tied shall, if practicable, sail a deciding race; if not, either the tie shall be broken by a method established under rule 3.2(a)(ix), or the yachts so tied shall either receive equal prizes or share the prize.

12—Yacht Materially Prejudiced
When, upon the request of a yacht made within the time limit provided by rule 68.3(*e*), Protests, or when the Race Committee, upon its own initiative, decides that, through no fault of her own, the finishing position of a yacht has been materially prejudiced: by rendering assistance in accordance with rule 58, Rendering Assistance; by being disabled by another yacht which was required to keep clear; or by action or omission of the Race Committee; it may **cancel** or **abandon** the race or make such other arrangement as it deems equitable.

13— Races to be Re-Sailed
When a race is to be re-sailed:—

1. All yachts entered in the original race shall be eligible to **start** in the race to be re-sailed.
2. Subject to the entry requirements of the original race, and at the discretion of the race committee, new entries may be accepted.
3. Rule infringements in the original race shall be disregarded for the purpose of **starting** in the race to be re-sailed.
4. The race committee shall notify the yachts concerned when and where the race will be re-sailed.

14—Award of Prizes, Places and Points
1. Before awarding the prizes, the Race Committee shall be satisfied that all yachts whose finishing positions affect the awards have observed the racing rules, the prescriptions of the National Authority, the sailing instructions and the class rules.

2. The sailing instructions may prescribe that in a particular instance the Race Committee may require the member in charge of a yacht to submit within a stated time limit a signed declaration to the effect that "all the racing rules, the prescriptions of the National Authority, the sailing instructions and the class rules were observed in the race (or races) on (date or dates of race or races)." A yacht which fails to observe the above requirement may, at the discretion of the Race Committee, be disqualified, or regarded as having retired.

(Numbers 15, 16, and 17 are spare numbers.)

PART III   GENERAL REQUIREMENTS

Owner's Responsibilities for Qualifying his Yacht
A yacht intending to race *shall, to avoid subsequent disqualification, comply with the rules of Part III before her preparatory signal and, when applicable, while* racing.

18—Entries
☆   Entries shall be made as required by the notice of the race or by the sailing instructions.

19—Measurement Certificates
1. Every yacht entering a race shall hold such valid measurement or rating certificate as may be required by the National Authority or other duly authorized body, by her class rules, by the notice of the race, or by the sailing instructions.
2. It shall be the owner's responsibility to maintain his yacht in the condition upon which her certificate was based.
3. (*a*) If the owner of a yacht cannot produce such a certificate when required, he may be permitted to sign and lodge with the Race Committee, before she **starts,** a statement in the following form:

To the Secretary _____*Club*
UNDERTAKING TO PRODUCE CERTIFICATE
The yacht _____ *competes in the* _____
race on condition that a valid certificate previously issued by the authorized administrative body, or a true copy of it, is submitted to the Race Committee before the end of the series, and that she competes in the races(s) on the measurement or rating of that certificate.
Signed _____
(Owner or his representative)
Date _____

(*b*) In this event the sailing instructions may require that the owner shall lodge such a deposit as may be required by the National Authority, which may be forfeited if such certificate or true copy is not submitted to the Race Committee within the prescribed period.

20—Ownership of Yachts
1. Unless otherwise prescribed in the conditions of entry, a yacht shall be eligible to compete only when she is either owned by or on charter to and has been entered by a yacht or sailing club recognized by a national authority or a member or members thereof.
2. Two or more yachts owned or chartered wholly or in part by the same body or person shall not compete in the same race without the previous consent of the race committee.

21—Member on Board
Every yacht shall have on board a member of a yacht or sailing club recognized by a national authority to be in charge of the yacht as owner or owner's representative.

22—Shifting Ballast
1. **General Restrictions.** Floorboards shall be kept down; bulkheads and doors left standing;

ladders, stairways and water tanks left in place; all cabin, galley and forecastle fixtures and fittings kept on board; all movable ballast shall be properly stowed under the floorboards or in lockers and no dead weight shall be shifted.

2. Shipping, Unshipping or Shifting Ballast; Water. No ballast, whether movable or fixed, shall be shipped, unshipped or shifted, nor shall any water be taken in or discharged except for ordinary ship's use, from 2100 hours on the day before the race until the yacht is no longer **racing**, except that bilge water may be removed at any time.

3. **Clothing and Equipment.**

(*a*) A competitor shall not wear or carry any clothing or equipment for the purpose of increasing his weight.

(*b*) A class which desires to make exception to rule 22.3(*a*), Clothing and Equipment, may so prescribe in its class rules. In so doing, however, the total weight of clothing and equipment worn or carried by a competitor shall not exceed twenty kilograms when wet.

23—Anchor

Unless otherwise prescribed by her class rules, every yacht shall carry on board an anchor and chain or rope of suitable size.

24—Life-Saving Equipment

☆ Every yacht shall carry life-saving equipment conforming to government regulations for all persons on board, one item of which shall be ready for immediate use.

25—Class Emblems, National Letters and Distinguishing Numbers

1. Every yacht of an international class recognized by the I.Y.R.U. shall carry on her mainsail, or as provided in (*d*) (iii) and (iv) on her spinnaker:—

(*a*) A emblem, letter or number denoting the class to which she belongs.

(*b*) When racing in foreign waters a letter or letters showing her nationality, thus:—

A	Argentine		IND	India
AL	Algeria		IR	Republic of Ireland
AR	United Arab Rebublic		IS	Israel
B	Belgium		J	Japan
BA	Bahamas		K	United Kingdom
BL	Brazil		KA	Australia
BU	Bulgaria		KB	Bermuda
CA	Cambodia		KBA	Barbados
CB	Colombia		KC	Canada
CY	Republic of Sri Lanka		KG	Guyana
CZ	Czechoslovakia		KGB	Gibraltar
D	Denmark		KH	Hong Kong
DR	Dominican Republic		KJ	Jamaica
E	Spain		KK	Kenya
EC	Ecuador		KR	Rhodesia
F	France		KS	Singapore
G	Federal Rupublic of Germany		KT	Trinidad and Tobago
GO	German Democratic Republic		KZ	New Zealand
			KZA	Zambia
GR	Greece		L	Finland
GU	Guatemala		LE	Lebanon
H	Holland		LX	Luxembourg
HA	Netherland Antilles		M	Hungary
I	Italy		MA	Morocco
IL	Iceland		MG	Madagascar
			MO	Monaco

MT	Malta		SA	Republic of South Africa
MX	Mexico		SE	Senegal
MY	Malasia		SL	El Salvador
N	Norway		SR	Union of Soviet Socialist
NK	Democratic People's Republic			Republics
	of Korea		T	Tunisia
OE	Austria		TA	Republic of China (Taiwan)
P	Portugal		TH	Thailand
PH	The Philippines		TK	Turkey
PK	Pakistan		U	Uruguay
PR	Puerto Rico		US	United States of America
PU	Peru		V	Venezuela
PZ	Poland		VI	U.S. Virgin Is.
RC	Cuba		X	Chile
RI	Indonesia		Y	Yugoslavia
RM	Roumania		Z	Switzerland
S	Sweden			

(c) Distinguishing number:—

A distinguishing number allotted to her by her own national authority. In the case of a self-administered international class, the number may be allotted by the class owners' association.

Assuming a Flying Dutchman yacht belonging to the Argentine Republic to be allotted number 3 by the Argentine National Authority, her sail shall be marked:

FD

A3

When there is insufficient space to place the letter or letters showing the yacht's nationality in front of her allotted number, it shall be placed above the number.

(d) (i) The class emblems, letters or number, national letters and distinguishing numbers shall be grouped so that the center of the group is above half height; shall sharply contrast in color with the sail; and shall be placed at different heights on the two sides of the sail, those on the starboard side being uppermost, to avoid confusion owing to translucency of the sail.

(ii) Where the class emblem, letter or number is of such a design that when placed back to back on the two sides of the sail they coincide, they may be so placed.

(iii) When **racing** in foreign waters, the national letters and distinguishing numbers only shall be similarly placed on both sides of the spinnaker, but at approximately half height.

(iv) When **racing** in home waters, the distinguishing numbers only need be placed in accordance with rule 25.1(d) (iii).

(e) The following minimum sizes for national letters and distinguishing numbers are prescribed:—

Height: one-tenth of the measurement of the foot of the mainsail rounded up to the nearest 50 mm.

Width: (excluding figure 1 and letter I) 70% of the height.

Thickness: 15% of the height.

Space between adjoining letters and numbers: 20% of the height. Classes which have a variable sail plan shall specify in their class rules the sizes of letters and numbers, which shall, if practicable, conform to the above requirements.

☆ 2(a) Unless otherwise authorized by the Race Committee or provided by class rules, a yacht not in one of the classes above shall carry her class number, letter or emblem and her racing number on her mainsail and spinnaker, as provided above, except that the only size requirement may be as an alternative that the numbers, letters and emblems shall be not less than 10 inches in height for yachts under 22 feet waterline length, not less than 15 inches in height for yachts 22 feet to 32 feet waterline and not less than 18 inches in height for yachts over 32 feet waterline length.

☆ (*b*) Offshore racing yachts shall carry N.A.Y.R.U. numbers on mainsails, spinnakers and all overlapping headsails whose LP measurement exceeds 130%.

3. A yacht shall not be disqualified for failing to comply with the provisions of rule 25 without prior warning and adequate opportunity to make correction.

26—Advertisements

1. The hull, crew or equipment of a yacht shall not display any form of advertisement except that:—

(*a*) One sailmaker's mark (which may include the name or mark of the manufacturer of the sail cloth) may be displayed on each side of any sail. The whole of such mark shall be placed not more than 15% of the length of the foot of the sail or 300 mm from its tack whichever is the greater. This latter limitation shall not apply to the position of marks on spinnakers.

(*b*) One builder's mark (which may include the name or mark of the designer) may be placed on the hull, and one maker's mark may be displayed on spars and equipment.

2. Marks (or plates) shall fit within a square not exceeding 150 mm × 150 mm (6 × 6 ins).

3. A yacht shall not be disqualified for infringing the provisions of this rule without prior warning and adequate opportunity to make correction.

27—Forestays and Jib Tacks

Unless otherwise prescribed in the class rules, forestays and jib tacks (excluding spinnaker staysails when not **close-hauled**) shall be fixed approximately in the center-line of the yacht.

28—Flags

☆ A yacht may display her private signal on the leech of her mainsail or from her mizzen mast head, and a wind indicator of a solid color or a feather. Other flags shall not be displayed except for signaling. A yacht shall not be disqualified for failing to comply with the provisions of this rule without warning and adequate opportunity to make correction.

(Numbers 29 and 30 are spare numbers.)

PART IV   SAILING RULES WHEN YACHTS MEET

Helmsman's Rights and Obligations Concerning Right of Way

The rules of Part IV apply only between yachts which either are intending to race *or are* racing *in the same or different races, and, except when rule 3.2(b)(ii) applies, replace the International Regulations for Preventing Collisions at Sea or Government Right-of-Way Rules applicable to the area concerned, from the time a yacht intending to* race *begins to sail about in the vicinity of the starting line until she has either* finished *or retired and has left the vicinity of the course.*

Section A—Rules Which Always Apply

31—Disqualification

1. A yacht may be disqualified or otherwise penalized for infringing a rule of Part IV only

when the infringement occurs while she is **racing**, whether or not a collision results.

2. A yacht may be disqualified before or after she is **racing** for seriously hindering a yacht which is **racing**, or for infringing the sailing instructions.

32—Avoiding Collisions

A right-of-way yacht which fails to make a reasonable attempt to avoid a collision resulting in serious damage may be disqualified as well as the other yacht.

33—Retiring from Race

A yacht which realizes she has infringed a racing rule or a sailing instruction is under an obligation to retire promptly; but, when she persists in **racing**, other yachts shall continue to accord her such rights as she may have under the rules of Part IV.

34—Right-of-Way Yacht Altering Course

When one yacht is required to keep clear of another, the right-of-way yacht shall not so alter course as to prevent the other yacht from keeping clear; so as to increase any alteration of course required of the other yacht in order to keep clear; or so as to obstruct her while she is keeping clear, except:

(*a*) to the extent permitted by rule 38.1, Right-of-Way Yacht Luffing after Starting, and

(*b*) when assuming a **proper course** to **start**, unless subject to the second part of rule 44.1(*b*), Yachts Returning to Start.

35—Hailing

1. Except when **luffing** under rule 38.1, Luffing after Starting, a right-of-way yacht which does not hail before or when making an alteration of course which may not be foreseen by the other yacht may be disqualified as well as the yacht required to keep clear when a collision resulting in serious damage occurs.

2. A yacht which hails when claiming the establishment or termination of an **overlap** or insufficiency of room at a **mark** or **obstruction** thereby helps to support her claim for the purposes of rule 42, Rounding or Passing Marks and Obstructions.

Section B—Opposite Tack Rule
36—Fundamental Rule

A **port-tack** yacht shall keep clear of a **starboard-tack** yacht.

Section C—Same Tack Rules
37—Fundamental Rules

1. A **windward yacht** shall keep clear of a **leeward yacht**.
2. A yacht **clear astern** shall keep clear of a yacht **clear ahead**.
3. A yacht which establishes an **overlap** to **leeward** from **clear astern** shall allow the **windward yacht** ample room and opportunity to keep clear, and during the existence of that **overlap** the **leeward yacht** shall not sail above her **proper course**.

38—Right-of-Way Yacht Luffing after Starting

1. **Luffing Rights and Limitations.** After she has **started** and cleared the starting line, a yacht **clear ahead** or a **leeward yacht** may **luff** as she pleases, except that:—

A leeward yacht shall not sail above her **proper course** while an **overlap** exists if, at any time during its existence, the helmsman of the **windward yacht** (when sighting abeam from his normal **station** and sailing no higher than the **leeward yacht**) has been abreast or forward of the mainmast of the **leeward yacht**.

2. **Overlap Limitations.** For the purpose of this rule: An **overlap** does not exist unless the yachts are clearly within two overall lengths of the longer yacht; and an **overlap**

which exists between two yachts when the leading yacht **starts**, or when one or both of them completes a **tack** or **jibe**, shall be regarded as a new **overlap** beginning at that time.

3. **Hailing to Stop or Prevent a Luff.** When there is doubt, the **leeward yacht** may assume that she has the right to **luff** unless the helmsman of the **windward yacht** has hailed "Mast Abeam", or words to that effect. The **leeward yacht** shall be governed by such hail, and, if she deems it improper, her only remedy is to protest.

4. **Curtailing a Luff.** The **windward yacht** shall not cause a **luff** to be curtailed because of her proximity to the **leeward yacht** unless an **obstruction**, a third yacht or other object restricts her ability to respond.

5. **Luffing Two or More Yachts.** A yacht shall not **luff** unless she has the right to **luff** all yachts which would be affected by her **luff**, in which case they shall all respond even if an intervening yacht or yachts would not otherwise have the right to **luff**.

39—Sailing Below a Proper Course

A yacht which on a free leg of the course shall not sail below her **proper course** when she is clearly within three of her overall lengths of either a **leeward yacht** or a yacht **clear astern** which is steering a course to pass to **leeward**.

40—Right-of-Way Yacht Luffing before Starting

Before a yacht has **started** and cleared the starting line, any **luff** on her part which causes another yacht to have to alter course to avoid a collision shall be carried out slowly and in such a way so as to give the **windward yacht** room and opportunity to keep **clear**, but the **leeward yacht** shall not so **luff** above a **close-hauled** course, unless the helmsman of the **windward yacht** (sighting abeam from his normal station) is abaft the mainmast of the **leeward yacht**. Rules 38.3, Hailing to Stop or Prevent a Luff; 38.4, Curtailing a Luff; and 38.5, Luffing Two or more Yachts, also apply.

Section D—Changing Tack Rules

41—Tacking or Jibing

1. A yacht which is either **tacking** or **jibing** shall keep clear of a yacht **on a tack**.

2. A yacht shall neither **tack** nor **jibe** into a position which will give her right of way unless she does so far enough from a yacht **on a tack** to enable this yacht to keep clear without having to begin to alter her course until after the **tack** or **jibe** has been completed.

3. A yacht which **tacks** or **jibes** has the onus of satisfying the race committee that she completed her **tack** or **jibe** in accordance with rule 41.2.

4. When two yachts are both **tacking** or both **jibing** at the same time, the one on the other's **port** side shall keep clear.

Section E—Rules of Exception and Special Application

When a rule of this section applies, to the extent to which it explicitly provides rights and obligations, it over-rides any conflicting rule of Part IV which precedes it except the rules of Section A—Rules Which Always Apply.

42—Rounding or Passing Marks and Obstructions

1. **Fundamental Rules Regarding Room.** When yachts either on the same **tack** or, after **starting** and clearing the starting line, on opposite **tacks**, are about to round or pass a **mark** on the same required side, with the exception of a starting **mark** surrounded by navigable water, or an **obstruction** on the same side:—

(a) **When Overlapped**

   (i) An outside yacht shall give each yacht **overlapping** her on the inside, room to round or pass the **mark** or **obstruction**, except as provided in rules 42.1(*a*)(iii), and (iv) and

42.3. Room includes room for an **overlapping** yacht to **tack** or **jibe** when either is an integral part of the rounding or passing manoeuvre.

(ii) When an inside yacht of two or more **overlapped** yachts either on opposite **tacks**, or on the same **tack** without **luffing** rights, will have to **jibe** in order most directly to assume a **proper course** to the next mark, she shall **jibe** at the first reasonable opportunity.

(iii) When two yachts on opposite **tacks** are on a beat or when one of them will have to **tack** either to round the **mark** or to avoid the **obstruction**, as between each other rule 42.1(a)(i) shall not apply and they are subject to rules 36, Opposite Tack Fundamental Rule, and 41, Tacking or Jibing.

(iv) An outside **leeward yacht** with **luffing** rights may take an inside yacht to windward of a **mark** provided that she hails to that effect and begins to **luff** before she is within two of her overall lengths of the **mark** and provided that she also passes to windward of it.

(b) **When Clear Astern and Clear Ahead**

(i) A yacht **clear astern** shall keep clear in anticipation of and during the rounding or passing manoeuvre when the yacht **clear ahead** remains on the same **tack** or **jibes**.

(ii) A yacht **clear ahead** which **tacks** to round a **mark** is subject to rule 41, Tacking or Jibing, but a yacht **clear astern** shall not **luff** above **close-hauled** so as to prevent the yacht **clear ahead** from **tacking**.

2. **Restrictions on Establishing and Maintaining an Overlap**

(a) A yacht **clear astern** shall not establish an inside **overlap** and be entitled to room under rule 42.1(a)(i) when the yacht **clear ahead**:—

(i) is within two of her overall lengths of the **mark** or **obstruction**, except as provided in rules 42.2(b) and 42.2(c); or

(ii) is unable to give the required room.

(b) The two-lengths determinative above shall not apply to yachts, of which one has completed a **tack** within two overall lengths of a **mark** or an **obstruction**.

(c) A yacht **clear astern** may establish an **overlap** between the yacht **clear ahead** and a continuing **obstruction** such as a shoal or the shore, only when there is room for her to do so in safety.

(d) (i) A yacht **clear ahead** shall be under no obligation to give room to a yacht **clear astern** before an **overlap** is established.

(ii) A yacht which claims an inside **overlap** has the onus of satifying the race committee that the **overlap** was established in proper time.

(e) (i) When an outside yacht is **overlapped** at the time she comes within two of her overall lengths of a **mark,** or an **obstruction**, she shall continue to be bound by rule 42.1(a)(i) to give room as required even though the **overlap** may thereafter be broken.

(ii) An outside yacht which claims to have broken an **overlap** has the onus of satisfying the race committee that she became **clear ahead** when she was more than two of her overall lengths from the **mark** or an **obstruction**.

3. **At a Starting Mark Surrounded by Navigable Water**

When approaching the starting line to **start**, a **leeward yacht** shall be under no obligation to give any **windward yacht** room to pass to leeward of a starting **mark** surrounded by navigable water; but, after the starting signal, a **leeward yacht** shall not deprive a **windward yacht** of room at such a **mark** by sailing either above the course to the first **mark** or above **close-hauled**.

43—Close-Hauled, Hailing for Room to Tack at Obstructions

1. **Hailing.** When two **close-hauled** yachts are on the same **tack** and safe pilotage requires the yacht **clear ahead** or the **leeward yacht** to make a substantial alteration of course to clear an **obstruction**, and if she intends to **tack**, but cannot **tack** without colliding with the other yacht, she shall hail the other yacht for room to **tack** and clear the other yacht, but she shall not hail and **tack** simultaneously.

56

2. Responding. The hailed yacht at the earliest possible moment after the hail shall either:—

(*a*) **tack**, in which case, the hailing yacht shall begin to **tack** either:—
    (i) before the hailed yacht has completed her **tack**,
    (ii) if she cannot then **tack** without colliding with the hailed yacht, immediately she is able to **tack** and clear her, or

(*b*) reply "You **tack**", or words to that effect, if in her opinion she can keep clear without **tacking** or after postponing her **tack**. In this case:—
    (i) the hailing yacht shall immediately **tack** and
    (ii) the hailed yacht shall keep clear.
    (iii) The onus shall lie on the hailed yacht which replied "You **tack**" to satisfy the race committee that she kept clear.

3. Limitation on Right to Room when the Obstruction is a Mark.

(*a*) When the hailed yacht can fetch an **obstruction** which is also a **mark**, the hailing yacht shall not be entitled to room to **tack** and clear the other yacht and the hailed yacht shall immediately so inform the hailing yacht.

(*b*) If, thereafter, the hailing yacht again hails for room to **tack** and clear the other yacht she shall, after receiving it, retire immediately.

(*c*) If, after having refused to respond to a hail under rule 43.3(a), the hailed yacht fails to fetch, she shall retire immediately.

44—Yachts Returning to Start

1. (*a*) A premature starter when returning to **start**, or a yacht working into position from the course side of the starting line or its extensions, when the starting signal is made, shall keep clear of all yachts which are **starting**, or have **started**, correctly, until she is wholly on the pre-start side of the starting line or its extensions.

(*b*) Thereafter, she shall be accorded the rights under the rules of Part IV of a yacht which is **starting** correctly; but if she thereby acquires right of way over another yacht which is **starting** correctly, she shall allow that yacht ample room and opportunity to keep clear.

2. A premature starter while continuing to sail the course and until it is obvious that she is returning to **start**, shall be accorded the rights under the rules of Part IV of a yacht which has **started**.

45—Yachts Re-rounding after Touching a Mark

1. A yacht which has touched a **mark** and is about to exonerate herself in accordance with rule 52.2, Touching a Mark, shall keep clear of all other yachts which are about to round or pass it or have rounded or passed it correctly, until she has rounded it completely and has cleared it and is on a **proper course** to the next **mark**.

2. A yacht which has touched a **mark**, while continuing to sail the course and until it is obvious that she is returning to round it completely in accordance with rule 52.2, Touching a Mark, shall be accorded rights under the rules of Part IV.

Section F—When Not Under Way
46—Anchored, Aground or Capsized

1. A yacht under way shall keep clear of another yacht **racing** which is anchored, aground or capsized. Of two anchored yachts, the one which anchored later shall keep clear, except that a yacht which is dragging shall keep clear of one which is not.

2. A yacht anchored or aground shall indicate the fact to any yacht which may be in danger of fouling her. Unless the size of the yachts or the weather conditions make some other signal necessary, a hail is sufficient indication.

3. A yacht shall not be penalized for fouling a yacht in distress which she is attempting to assist or a yacht which goes aground or capsizes immediately ahead of her.

(Numbers 47 and 48 are spare numbers.)

Obligations of Helmsman and Crew in Handling a Yacht

Except for rule 49, a yacht is subject to the rules of Part V only while she is **racing.**

49—Fair Sailing

A yacht shall attempt to win a race only by fair sailing, superior speed and skill, and, except in team races, by individual effort. However, a yacht may be disqualified under this rule only in the case of a clear-cut violation of the above principles and only if no other rule applies.

50—Ranking as a Starter

A yacht whose entry has been accepted by the Race Committee and which sails about in the vicinity of the starting line between her preparatory and starting signals shall rank as a starter, even if she does not **start.**

51—Sailing the Course

1.(*a*) A yacht shall **start** and **finish** only as prescribed in the starting and finishing definitions.

(*b*) Unless otherwise prescribed in the sailing instructions, a yacht which either crosses prematurely, or is on the course side of the starting line, or its extensions, at the starting signal, shall return and **start** in accordance with the definition.

(*c*) Unless otherwise prescribed in the sailing instructions, when after a general recall, any part of a yacht's hull, crew or equipment is on the course side of the starting line or its extensions during the minute before her starting signal, she shall thereafter return to the pre-start side of the line across one of its extensions and **start.**

(*d*) Failure of a yacht to see or hear her recall notification shall not relieve her of her obligation to **start** correctly.

2. A yacht shall sail the course so as to round or pass each **mark** on the required side in correct sequence, and so that a string representing her wake from the time she **starts** until she **finishes** would, when drawn taut, lie on the required side of each **mark.**

3. A **mark** has a required side for a yacht as long as she is on a leg which it begins, bounds or ends. A starting line **mark** begins to have a required side for a yacht when she **starts.** A starting limit **mark** has a required side for a yacht from the time she is approaching the starting line to **start** until she has left it astern on the first leg. A finishing line **mark** and a finishing limit **mark** cease to have a required side for a yacht as soon as she **finishes.**

4. A yacht which rounds or passes a **mark** on the wrong side may exonerate herself by making her course conform to the requirements of rule 51.2.

5. It is not necessary for a yacht to cross the finishing line completely; after **finishing** she may clear it in either direction.

☆ 6. In the absence of the Race Committee, a yacht shall take her own time when she **finishes,** and report the time taken to the Race Committee as soon as possible. If there is no longer an established finishing line, the finishing line shall be a line extending from the required side of the finishing **mark** at right angles to the last leg of the course, and 100 yards long or as much longer as may be necessary to insure adequate depth of water in crossing it.

52—Touching a Mark

1. A yacht which either:—

(*a*) touches:—

(i) a starting **mark** before **starting;**

(ii) a **mark** which begins, bounds or ends the leg of the course on which she is sailing; or

(iii) a finishing **mark** after **finishing,** or

(*b*) causes a **mark** or mark vessel to shift to avoid being touched, shall immediately retire, unless either:

(i) she alleges that she was wrongfully compelled by another yacht to touch it or cause it to shift, in which case she shall protest; or

(ii) she exonerates herself in accordance with rule 52.2.

2.(*a*) Unless otherwise prescribed in the sailing instructions, a yacht which touches a **mark** surrounded by navigable water may exonerate herself by completing one entire rounding of the **mark**, leaving it on the required side, and thereafter she shall re-round or re-pass it, without touching it, as required to sail the course in accordance with rule 51, Sailing the Course, and the sailing instructions.

(*b*) When a yacht touches:

(i) a starting **mark**, she shall carry out the rounding after she has **started**; or

(ii) a finishing **mark**, she shall carry out the rounding, and she shall not rank as having **finished** until she has completed the rounding and again crosses the finishing line in accordance with the definition of **finishing**.

53—Fog Signals and Lights

1. Every yacht shall observe the International Regulations for Preventing Collisions at Sea or Government Rules and fog signals and, as a minimum, the carrying of lights at night.

☆ 2. The use of additional special purpose lights such as masthead, spreader or jib luff lights shall not constitute grounds for protest.

54—Setting and Sheeting Sails

1. **Changing Sails.** While changing headsails and spinnakers a replacing sail may be fully set and trimmed before the sail it replaces is taken in, but only one mainsail and, except when changing, only one spinnaker shall be carried set.

2. **Sheeting Sails to Spars.** Unless otherwise prescribed by the class rules, any sail may be sheeted to or led above a boom regularly used for a working sail and permanently attached to the mast to which the head of the working sail is set, but no sails shall be sheeted over or through outriggers. An outrigger is any fitting so placed, except as permitted in the first sentence of rule 54.2, that it could exert outward pressure on a sheet at a point from which, with the yacht upright, a vertical line would fall outside the hull or deck planking at that point, or outside such other position as class rules prescribe. For the purpose of this rule: bulwarks, rails and rubbing strakes are not part of the hull or deck planking. A boom of a boomed headsail which requires no adjustment when **tacking** is not an outrigger.

3. **Spinnaker, Spinnaker Pole.** A spinnaker shall not be set without a pole. The tack of a spinnaker when set and drawing shall be in close proximity to the outboard end of a spinnaker pole. Any headsail may be attached to a spinnaker pole provided a spinnaker is not set. A sail tacked down abaft the foremost mast is not a headsail. Only one spinnaker pole shall be used at a time and when in use shall be carried only on the side of the foremost mast opposite to the main boom and shall be fixed to the mast. Rule 54.3 shall not apply when shifting a spinnaker pole or sail attached thereto.

55—Owner Steering Another Yacht

An owner shall not steer any yacht other than his own in a race wherein his own yacht competes, without the previous consent of the race committee.

56—Boarding

Unless otherwise prescribed in the sailing instructions, no person shall board a yacht except for the purpose of rule 58, Rendering Assistance, or to attend an injured or ill member of the crew or temporarily as one of the crew of a vessel fouled.

57—Leaving, Man Overboard

Unless otherwise prescribed in the sailing instructions, no person on board a yacht when her preparatory signal was made shall leave, unless injured or ill, or for the purposes of rule 58, Rendering Assistance, except that any member of the crew may fall overboard or leave her to swim, stand on the bottom as a means of anchoring, haul her out ashore to effect repairs, reef sails or bail out, or help her to get clear after grounding or fouling another vessel or object, provided that this person is back on board before the yacht continues in the race.

58—Rendering Assistance
Every yacht shall render all possible assistance to any vessel or person in peril, when in a position to do so.

59—Outside Assistance
Except as permitted by rules 56, Boarding, 58, Rendering Assistance, and 64, Aground or Foul of an Obstruction, a yacht shall neither receive outside assistance nor use any gear other than that on board when her preparatory signal was made.

60—Means of Propulsion
A yacht shall be propelled only by the natural action of the wind on the sails, spars and hull, and water on the hull, and shall not pump, "ooch" or rock, as described in Appendix 2, nor check way by abnormal means, except for the purpose of rule 58, Rendering Assistance, or of recovering a man who has accidentally fallen overboard. An oar, paddle or other object may be used in emergency for steering. An anchor may be sent out in a boat only as permitted by rule 64, Aground or Foul of an Obstruction.

61—Sounding
Any means of sounding may be used provided rule 60, Means of Propulsion, is not infringed.

62—Manual Power
A yacht shall use manual power only, except that a power winch or windlass may be used in weighing anchor or in getting clear after running aground or fouling any object, and a power bilge pump may be used in an auxiliary yacht.

63—Anchoring and Making Fast
1. A yacht may anchor. Means of anchoring may include the crew standing on the bottom and any weight lowered to the bottom. A yacht shall recover any anchor or weight used, and any chain or rope attached to it, before continuing in the race, unless after making every effort she finds recovery impossible. In this case she shall report the circumstances to the race committee, which may disqualify her if it considers the loss due either to inadequate gear or to insufficient effort to recover it.
2. A yacht shall be afloat and off moorings, before her preparatory signal, but may be anchored, and shall not thereafter make fast or be made fast by means other than anchoring, nor be hauled out, except for the purpose of rule 64, Aground or Foul of an Obstruction, or to effect repairs, reef sails or bail out.

64—Aground or Foul of an Obstruction
A yacht, after grounding or fouling another vessel or other object, is subject to rule 62, Manual Power, and may, in getting clear, use her own anchors, boats, ropes, spars and other gear; may send out an anchor in a boat; may be refloated by her crew going overboard either to stand on the bottom or to go ashore to push off; but may receive outside assistance only from the crew of the vessel fouled. A yacht shall recover all her own gear used in getting clear before continuing in the race.

65—Skin Friction
A yacht shall not eject or release from a container any substance (such as polymer) the purpose of which is, or could be, to reduce the frictional resistance of the hull by altering the character of the flow of water inside the boundary layer.

66—Increasing Stability

Unless otherwise prescribed by her class rules or in the sailing instructions, a yacht shall not use any device, such as a trapeze or plank, to project outboard the weight of any of the crew, nor, when a yacht is equipped with lifelines, shall any member of the crew station any part of his torso outside them, other than temporarily.

PART VI   PROTESTS, DISQUALIFICATIONS AND APPEALS

67—Contact between Yachts Racing

1. When there is contact between the hull, spars, standing rigging or crew of two yachts while racing, both shall be disqualified, unless one of them retires in acknowledgement of an infringement of the rules, or one or both of them acts in accordance with rule 68.3, Protests.
2. A third yacht which witnesses an apparent collision between two yachts and, after finishing or retiring, discovers that neither of them has observed rule 67.1, is relieved by rule 68.3(b) from the requirement of showing a protest flag and may lodge a protest against them.
3. The Race Committee may waive this rule when it is satisfied that minor contact was unavoidable.

68—Protests

1. A yacht can protest against any other yacht, except that a protest for an alleged infringement of the rules of Part IV can be made only by a yacht directly involved in, or witnessing an incident.
2. A protest occurring between yachts competing in separate races sponsored by different clubs shall be heard by a combined committee of both clubs.
3. (a) A protest for an infringement of the rules or sailing instructions occurring during a race shall be signified by showing a flag (International Code flag "B" is always acceptable, irrespective of any other provisions in the sailing instructions) conspicuously in the rigging of the protesting yacht at the first reasonable opportunity and keeping it flying until she has finished or retired, or if the first reasonable opportunity occurs after finishing, until acknowledged by the race committee. In the case of a yacht sailed single-handed, it will be sufficient if the flag (whether displayed in the rigging or not) is brought to the notice of the yacht protested against as soon as possible after the incident and to the race committee when the protesting yacht finishes.

(b) A yacht which has no knowledge of the facts justifying a protest until after she has finished or retired may nevertheless protest without having shown a protest flag.

(c) A protesting yacht shall try to inform the yacht protested against that a protest will be lodged.

(d) Such a protest shall be in writing and be signed by the owner or his representative, and include the following particulars:

    (i) The date, time and whereabouts of the incident.

    (ii) The particular rule or rules or sailing instructions alleged to have been infringed.

    (iii) A statement of the facts.

    (iv) Unless irrelevant, a diagram of the incident.

(e) Unless otherwise-prescribed in the sailing instructions a protesting yacht shall deliver, or if that is not possible, mail her protest to the race committee:

    (i) within two hours of the time she finishes the race, or within such time as may have been prescribed in the sailing instructions under rule 3.2(b)(xv), unless the race committee has reason to extend these time limits, or

    (ii) When she does not finish the race, within such a time as the race committee may consider reasonable in the circumstances of the case. A protest shall be accompanied by such fee, if any, as may have been prescribed in the sailing instructions under rule 3.2(b)(xv).

(f) The Race Committee shall allow the protestor to remedy at a later time:

(i) any defects in the details required by rule 68.3*(d)* provided that the protest includes a summary of the facts, and

(ii) a failure to deposit such fee as may be required under rule 68.3*(e)* and prescribed in the sailing instructions.

4.*(a)* A protest that a measurement, scantling or flotation rule has been infringed while **racing,** or that a classification or rating certificate is for any reason invalid, shall be lodged with the race committee not later than 1800 hours on the day following the race. The race committee shall send a copy of the protest to the yacht protested against and, when there appears to be reasonable grounds for the protest, it shall refer the question to an authority qualified to decide such questions. (See Appendix 6).

(b) Deviations in excess of tolerances stated in the class rules caused by normal wear or damage and which do not affect the performance of the yacht shall not invalidate the measurement or rating certificate of the yacht for a particular race, but shall be rectified before she **races** again, unless in the opinion of the Race Committee there has been no practical opportunity to rectify the wear or damage.

(c) The Race Committee, in making its decision, shall be governed by the determination of such authority. Copies of such decision shall be sent to all yachts involved.

5.*(a)* A yacht which alleges that her chances of winning a prize have been prejudiced by an action or omission of the Race Committee, may seek redress from the Race Committee in accordance with the requirements for a protest provided in rules 68.3*(d)*, *(e)* and *(f)*. In these circumstances a protest flag need not be shown.

(b) **When the race committee decides that such action or omission was prejudicial, and that the result of the race was altered thereby, it shall cancel or abandon the race, or make such other arrangement as it deems equitable.**

6. A protest made in writing shall not be withdrawn, but shall be decided by the race committee, unless prior to the hearing full responsibility is acknowledged by one or more yachts.

7. Alternative Penalties. When so prescribed in the sailing instructions, the procedure and penalty for infringing a rule of Part IV shall be as provided in Appendix 3, Alternative Penalties for Infringement of a Rule of Part IV.

69—Refusal of a Protest

1. When the race committee decides that a protest does not conform to the requirements of rule 68, Protests, it shall inform the protesting yacht that her protest will not be heard and of the reasons for such decision.

2. Such a decision shall not be reached without giving the protesting yacht all opportunity of bringing evidence that the requirements of rule 68, Protests, were complied with.

70—Hearings

1. When the race committee decides that a protest conforms to all the requirements of rule 68, Protests, it shall call a hearing as soon as possible. The protest, or a copy of it, shall be made available to all yachts involved, and each shall be notified, in writing if practicable, of the time and place set for the hearing. A reasonable time shall be allowed for the preparation of defense. At the hearing, the race committee shall take the evidence presented by the parties to the protest and such other evidence as it may consider necessary. The parties to the protest, or a representative of each, shall have the right to be present, but all others, except one witness at a time while testifying, may be excluded. A yacht other than one named in the protest, which is involved in that protest, shall have all the privileges of yachts originally named in it.

2. A yacht shall not be penalized without a hearing, except as provided in rule 73.1(a), Disqualification without Protest.

3. Failure on the part of any of the interested parties or a representative to make an effort to attend the hearing of the protest may justify the race committee in deciding the protest as it thinks fit without a full hearing.

71—Decisions

The race committee shall make its decision promptly after the hearing. Each decision shall be communicated to the parties involved, and shall state fully the facts and grounds on which it is based and shall specify the rules, if any, infringed. If requested by any of the parties, such decision shall be given in writing and shall include the race committee's diagram. The findings of the race committee as to the facts involved shall be final.

72—Disqualifications after Protest

1. When the race committee, after hearing a protest or acting under rule 73, Disqualification without Protest, or any appeal authority, is satisfied:—

(*a*) that a yacht has infringed any of these rules or the sailing instructions, or

(*b*) that in consequence of her neglect of any of these rules or the sailing instructions she has compelled other yachts to infringe any of these rules or the sailing instructions,

she shall be disqualified unless the sailing instructions applicable to that race provide some other penalty. Such disqualification or other penalty shall be imposed, irrespective of whether the rule or sailing instruction which led to the disqualification or penalty was mentioned in the protest, or the yacht which was at fault was mentioned or protested against, e.g., the protesting yacht or a third yacht might be disqualified and the protested yacht absolved.

2. For the purpose of awarding points in a series, a retirement after an infringement of any of these rules or the sailing instructions shall not rank as a disqualification. This penalty can be imposed only in accordance with rules 72, Disqualification after Protest, and 73, Disqualification without Protest.

3. When a yacht either is disqualified or has retired, the next in order shall be awarded her place.

73—Disqualification without Protest

1.(*a*) A yacht which fails either to **start** or **finish** may be disqualified without protest or hearing, after the conclusion of the race, except that she shall be entitled to a hearing, provided she satisfies the race committee that an error may have been made.

(*b*) A yacht so penalized shall be informed of the action taken, either by letter or by notification in the racing results.

2. When the race committee:—

(*a*) sees an apparent infringement by a yacht of any of these rules or the sailing instructions (except as provided in rule 73.1), or

(*b*) has reasonable grounds for believing that an infringement resulted in serious damage, or

(*c*) receives a report not later than the same day from a witness who was neither competing in the race, nor otherwise an interested party, alleging an infringement, or

(*d*) has reasonable grounds for supposing from the evidence at the hearing of a valid protest, that any yacht involved in the incident may have committed such an infringement,

it may notify such yacht thereof orally, or if that is not possible, in writing, delivered or mailed not later than 1800 hours on the day after:—

    (i) the finish of the race, or

    (ii) the receipt of the report, or

    (iii) the hearing of the protest.

Such notice shall contain a statement of the pertinent facts and of the particular rule or rules or sailing instructions believed to have been infringed, and the race committee shall act thereon in the same manner as if it had been a protest made by a competitor.

74—Penalties for Gross Infringement of Rules

1. When a gross infringement of any of these rules, the sailing instructions or class rules is proved against the owner, the owner's representative, the helmsman or sailing master of a yacht, such persons may be disqualified by the National Authority, for any period it may think fit, from either steering or sailing in a yacht in any race held under its jurisdiction.

2. Notice of any penalty adjudged under this rule shall be communicated to the I.Y.R.U. which shall inform all national authorities.

3. After a gross breach of good manners or sportsmanship the Race Committee may exclude a competitor from further participation in a series or take other disciplinary action.

75—Persons Interested not to take part in Decision

1. No member of either a Race Committee or of any appeals authority shall take part in the discussion or decision upon any disputed question in which he is an interested party, but this does not preclude him from giving evidence in such a case.

2. The term "interested party" includes anyone who stands to gain or lose as a result of the decision.

76—Expenses Incurred by Protest

Unless otherwise prescribed by the race committee, the fees and expenses entailed by a protest on measurement or classification shall be paid by the unsuccessful party.

77—Appeals

☆ 1. Limitations on Right to Appeal—Appeals involving solely the interpretation of the racing rules may be taken to the Appeals Committee of the Union for final determination:

a. If the Club is a member of the Union but is not a member of a local association or district belonging to the Union, by an owner or his representative from a decision of the Race Committee;

b. If the Club is a member of a local association or district belonging to the Union by an owner or his representative or by the Race Committee from a decision of the local association or district.

2. **Appeal Procedure**

a. A notice of appeal shall be mailed, not later than ten days from receipt of the written decision, to the body rendering the decision, preferably with a copy to the Appeals Committee, and shall contain the grounds for the appeal, that is to say, how the appellant believes the rules should be interpreted and his reasons therefor.

b. The body rendering the decision shall promptly notify the other parties involved, sending them a copy of the notice of appeal.

c. In an appeal to the Union the body rendering the decision shall promptly file, in writing, with the Secretary of the Union all particulars called for by rule 78, Particulars to be Provided in Appeals.

3. Decision of Appeals Committee—Decisions of the Appeals Committee shall be in writing and the grounds of each decision shall be specified therein. Each decision shall be filed with the Secretary of the Union, who shall send copies thereof to all parties to the infringement and appeal.

☆ 78—Particulars to be Supplied in Appeals

An appeal to the Union shall include the following particulars so far as they are applicable:
1. A copy of the protest or protests, request for relief or statement by the Race Committee acting under rule 73.2, as the case may be, together with all other written statements which may have been put in by the parties.
2. The names or numbers of the yachts represented at the hearing, and of any yacht duly notified of the hearing, but not represented, and the name and address of the representative of each of said yachts.
3. A copy of the sailing instructions.
4. A copy of the decision of the Race Committee containing a .full statement of the facts found by it, its decision and the grounds therefor.
5. An official diagram prepared by the Race Committee in accordance with the facts found by it and signed by it and showing (i) the course to the next **mark** or, if close by, the **mark** itself and its required side, (ii) the direction and velocity of the wind, (iii) the set of the current, if any, and (iv) the position or positions and tracks of the **yachts** involved.
6. A copy of the decision, if any, of the local association or district.

7. A copy of the notice of appeal, including the grounds thereof.

8. Observations, if any, upon the appeal by any of the parties.

☆ 79—Questions of Interpretation

The Appeals Committee will accept and act upon questions involving solely the interpretation of the racing rules but only when submitted by a club or local association or district, from whose decision an appeal may be taken as provided in rule 77.1, Limitations on Right to Appeal. Decisions of such questions may, at the discretion of the Chairman of the Appeals Committee, be acted upon by less than the full committee. Questions should include all the assumed facts, an assumed sailing instruction if pertinent, and a diagram if one will help to clarify the facts. Questions are not acceptable on protest decisions which may be appealed.

TEAM RACING RULES

Team racing shall be sailed under the yacht racing rules of the International Yacht Racing Union as adopted by the North American Yacht Racing Union supplemented as follows:

Sailing Rules

1. A yacht may manoeuvre against a yacht sailing on another leg of the course only if she can do so while sailing a **proper course** relative to the leg on which she herself is sailing. For the purpose of this rule, each time a leg is sailed it shall be regarded as "another **leg** of the course".

2. Except to protect her own or a team mate's finishing position, a yacht in one team which is completing the last leg of the course shall not manoeuvre against a yacht in another team which has no opponent astern of her.

3. Right of way may be waived by team mates, provided that in so doing, I.Y.R.U. rule 34, Right-of-Way Yacht Altering Course, is not infringed in respect to an opponent; but if contact occurs between them and neither retires immediately, the poorer finishing team mate shall automatically be disqualified.

The benefits of rule 12, Yacht Materially Prejudiced, shall not be available to a yacht damaged by contact between team mates.

4. When two **overlapping** yachts on the same **tack** are in the act of rounding or passing on the required side of a **mark** at which their **proper course** changes:

(a) If the **leeward** yacht is inside, she may, if she has **luffing** rights hold her course or **luff.** If she does not have **luffing** rights, she shall promptly assume her **proper course** to the next **mark** whether or not she has to **jibe:**

(b) If the **windward yacht** is inside, she shall promptly **luff** up to her **proper course** to the next **mark,** or if she cannot assume such **proper course** without **tacking** and does not choose to **tack,** she shall promptly **luff** up to **close-hauled.** This clause does not restrict a **leeward yacht's** right to **luff** under rule 38, Luffing after Starting.

Scoring

5. Each Race

(a) Yachts shall score three-quarters of a point for first place, two points for second place, three points for third place, and so on.

(b) A yacht which does not **start** shall score points equal to the number of yachts entitled to **start** in the race.

(c) A yacht which infringes any rule and retires with reasonable promptness shall score one point more than the number of yachts entitled to **start** in the race, but if her retirement is tardy, or if she fails to retire and is subsequently disqualified, she shall score four points more than the number of yachts entitled to **start** in the race.

(d) A yacht which infringes a rule shortly before or when **finishing** shall be considered to have retired with reasonable promptness if she notifies the race committee of her retirement as soon as is reasonably practicable.

(e) A yacht which does not **finish** for a reason other than an infringement shall score points equal to the number of yachts entitled to **start** in the race, except as provided in (*f*).

(f) After all the yachts of one team have **finished** or retired, the Race Committee may stop the race and award to each yacht of the other team which is still **racing** and underway the points she would have received had she **finished.**

(g) The team with the lowest total point score shall be the winner of the race.

6. Reports and Declarations

(*a*) A yacht which retires shall promptly report that fact and the reason therefor to the Race Committee, and if it resulted from a rule infringement she shall state:

    (i) when the infringement occurred;

    (ii) which yacht(s), if any, was involved in the infringement; and

    (iii) when she retired.

The sailing instructions may require her to submit within a prescribed time a signed statement covering (i), (ii) and (iii).

(*b*) The sailing instructions may require a yacht to sign a declaration within a prescribed time in accordance with rule 14, Award of Prizes, Places and Points.

(*c*) A yacht which fails either:

    (i) to report her retirement in accordance with rule 6(*a*) above; or

    (ii) to sign such declaration as may be required under rule 6(*b*) above, shall be awarded points on the assumption that she retired tardily owing to a rule infringement.

☆ 7. The Match and Breaking Ties

(*a*) When two teams only are competing: ·

    (i) the team winning the greater number of races shall be the winner of the match.

    (ii) When there is a tie because each team has won the same number of races it shall be resolved in favor of the winner of the last race.

(*b*) When more than two teams are competing in a series consisting of races each of which is between two teams:

    (i) The team winning the greatest number of races shall be the winner of the match.

    (ii) When there is a tie because two or more teams have won the same number of races, the winner shall be the team which has beaten the other tied team or teams in the most races, or if still tied, the team with the lowest point score, or if still tied, the team which beat the other in the last race between them.

(*c*) When more than two teams are all competing in each race:

    (i) The team with the lowest total point score in all races sailed shall be the winner of the match.

    (ii) When there is a tie the winner shall be the team which has beaten the other tied team or teams in the most races, or if still tied, the team which beat the other team or teams in the last race.

(*d*) Notwithstanding the above provisions for breaking ties, a tie shall instead be resolved by a sail-off, if practicable, in which case the time for the sail-off shall be scheduled before the series starts.

Addendum
Rules Recommended to Apply When the Home Team Provides All Racing Yachts.

A. ALLOTMENT OF YACHTS. The home team shall provide the visiting team with a list of the yachts to be used and of the sail numbers allotted to each yacht for the match. The home team shall divide these yachts into as many equal groups as there are competing teams and these groups shall be drawn for by lot for the first race. The yachts shall then be allotted to the crews by each team, except that a helmsman shall not at any time steer the yacht of which he is normally the helmsman. The groups of yachts shall be exchanged between races so that, as far as possible, each group will be sailed in turn by each team. In a two team match after an even number of races, if either team requests that the yachts be regrouped, the home team shall re-divide them into new groups which shall be drawn for by lot; except that for the final odd race of a two team match, the visiting team may select the group it wishes to sail.

B. ALLOTMENT OF SAILS. If sails as well as yachts are provided by the home team, the sails used by each yacht in the first race shall be used by her throughout the series and the substitution of a spare or extra sail shall not be permitted unless because of damage or for some other valid reason, a change is approved by the Race Committee after notification to both teams.

C. GROUP IDENTIFICATION: One group shall carry no markings. The second group shall carry dark colored strips or pennants, and additional groups shall carry light or differently colored strips or pennants. Strips or pennants should usually be provided by the home team and should be attached to the same conspicuous place on each boat of a group, such as the after end of the main boom or permanent backstay.

D. BREAKDOWNS: When a breakdown results in substantial loss, the Race Committee shall decide whether or not it was the fault of the crew. In general, a breakdown caused by defective equipment, or the result of a foul by an opponent shall not be deemed the fault of the crew, and a breakdown caused by careless handling or capsizing shall be. In case of doubt, the doubt shall be resolved in favor of the crew.

E. If the Race Committee decides that the breakdown was not the fault of the crew and that a reasonably competent crew could not have remedied the defect in time to prevent substantial loss, it shall cancel the race, or order it to be resailed, or award the breakdown yacht the number of points she would have received had she finished in the same position in the race she held when she broke down. In case of doubt as to her position when she broke down, the doubt shall be resolved against her.

F. SPARES: The home team shall be prepared to provide one or more extra yachts and sails to replace any which, in the opinion of the Race Committee, are unfit for use in the remaining races.

APPENDIX I

Amateur

1. For the purpose of international yacht races in which yachts entering are required to have one or more amateurs on board, and in other races with similar requirements, an amateur is a yachtsman who engages in yacht racing as a pastime as distinguished from a means of obtaining a livelihood. No yachtsman shall lose amateur status by reason of the fact that his livelihood is derived from designing or constructing any boats or parts of boats, or accessories of boats, or sails or from other professions associated with the sea and ships.

2. Any yachtsman whose amateur status is questioned or is in doubt, may apply to the national authority of the country of his residence for recognition of his amateur status. Any such applicant may be required to provide such particulars and evidence and to pay such fee as the national authority may prescribe. Recognition may be suspended or cancelled by the national authority by which it was granted.

3. The permanent committee of the International Yacht Racing Union, or any tribunal nominated by the chairman of that committee, may review the decision of any authority as to the amateur status of a yachtsman for the purpose of competing in international races.

4. For the purposes of participation in the Olympic Regatta an amateur is required to conform to the eligibility rules of the International Olympic Committee. Information on these eligibility requirements is available from all national authorities.

APPENDIX II

"Pumping" Sails, "Ooching" and "Rocking"

"Pumping" consists of frequent rapid trimming of sails with no particular reference to a change in true or apparent wind direction. To promote planing or surfing, rapid trimming of sails need not be considered "pumping."

The purpose of this interpretation of rule 60 is to prevent "fanning" one's boat around the course by flapping the sail similar to a bird's wing in flight. "Pumping" or **frequent,** quickly-repeated trimming and releasing of the mainsail to increase propulsion is not allowed and is not "the natural action of the wind on the sails."

Similarly, frequent, quickly-repeated jibing or roll-tacking in calm and near calm conditions fall into the same category as "pumping".

Where surfing or planing conditions exist, however, rule 60 allows taking advantage of "the natural action of water on the hull" through the **rapid** trimming of sails and adjustment of helm to **promote** (initiate) surfing or planing.

The test is whether or not the conditions are such that by **rapid** trimming of sails a boat could be **started** surfing or planing. A skipper challenged for "pumping" will have to prove, through the performance either of his own boat or of other boats, that surfing or planing conditions existed, and that the **frequency** of his **rapid** trimming was geared to the **irregular** or **cyclical** wave forms rather than to a **regular** rhythmic pattern.

Note that the interpretation refers to "promoting" and not to "maintaining" surfing or planing. Once a boat has started surfing or planing on a particular set of wave forms, from then on she must let the natural action of wind and water propel her without further **rapid** trimming and releasing of the sails.

Rapid trimming when approaching marks or the finishing line or other critical points should be consistent with that which was practiced throughout the leg.

"Ooching", which consists of lunging forward and stopping abruptly, falls in the same category as "pumping."

"Rocking" consists of persistently rolling a yacht from side to side.

APPENDIX III

Alternative Penalties for Infringement of a Rule of Part IV

Experience indicates that the 720° turns penalty is most satisfactory for small boats in relatively short races and it can be dangerous for large boats and not sufficiently severe in long races. The 20% penalty is relatively mild and is designed to encourage acknowledgement of infringements and willingness to protest when not acknowledged. Graduated penalties assign heavier penalties for more serious infringements. All three systems keep yachts racing.

Any one of the three following alternatives to disqualification may be used by including in the sailing instructions a provision such as the following (or if preferred the selected penalty may be quoted in full):—

The 720° turns penalty (or the percentage penalty or graduated penalties) as provided in Appendix 3 of the yacht racing rules will apply instead of disqualification, for infringement of a rule of Part IV.

720° Turns

A yacht which acknowledges infringing a rule of Part IV may exonerate herself by making two full 360° turns (720°) subject to the following provisions:

1. The yacht infringed against shall notify the infringing yacht at the first reasonable opportunity by hail and by showing a protest flag. (The first reasonable opportunity for a hail is usually immediately.)

2. Upon such notification, the yacht acknowledging fault shall immediately start to get well clear of other yachts and while on the same leg of the course she shall hail adjacent yachts of her intention and then make her turns. While so doing, she shall keep clear of all other yachts until she has completed her turns and is on a **proper course** to the next **mark.**

3. For the purpose of applying this penalty, "a leg of the course" shall be deemed terminated when two boat lengths from the **mark** ending that leg, and the next leg shall be deemed to commence at this point except for the final leg which is terminated when a yacht is no longer **racing.**

4. The turns may be made in either direction but both in the same direction.

5. When the infringement occurs before the starting signal, the infringing yacht shall make her turns after the starting signal and before **starting.**

6. When an infringement occurs at the finishing line, the infringing yacht shall make her turns on the last leg of the course before being officially finished.

7. If neither yacht acknowledges fault, a protest may be lodged in accordance with rule 68, Protests, and the sailing instructions.

8. An infringing yacht shall report her infringement and the resulting action taken by her to the Race Committee, together with such other information as may be required by the sailing instructions.

9. Failure to observe the above requirements will render a yacht which has infringed a rule of Part IV liable to disqualification or other penalty.

10. An infringing yacht involved in a collision which results in serious damage to either yacht shall be liable to disqualification.

Percentage

1. A yacht which acknowledges infringing a rule of Part IV shall be penalized by receiving the score for the place worse than her actual finishing position by 20% to the nearest whole number of the number of starters in that race, except that the penalty shall be at least three places and except further that in no case will she receive a score for a position worse than one more than the number of starters. (Examples: An infringing yacht which finishes eighth in a start of nineteen yachts will receive the score for twelfth place ($19 \times 0.2 = 3.8$ or 4); an infringing yacht which finishes thirteenth in a start of fourteen yachts will receive the score for fifteenth place.)

(*a*) A yacht infringing a rule in more than one incident shall receive a 20% penalty for each incident.

(*b*) The imposition of a 20% penalty on a yacht shall not affect the score of other yachts. (Thus two yachts may receive the same score.)

2. The yacht infringed against shall notify the infringing yacht at the first reasonable opportunity by hail and by showing a protest flag. (The first reasonable opportunity for a hail is usually immediately.)

3. A yacht which acknowledges infringing a rule of Part IV shall at the first reasonable opportunity show International Code flag "I", or such other signal as the sailing instructions may specify, keep it flying until she has finished and report the infringement to the Race Committee.

4. A yacht which fails to acknowledge an infringement as provided in paragraph 3 and which, after a protest and hearing, is found to have infringed a rule of Part IV, shall be penalized 30% or at least five places instead of 20%.

5. A yacht which has shown International Code flag "I" during a race and has not reported the infringement to the Race Committee shall be liable to the 30% penalty of paragraph 4 without a hearing except on the two points of having shown the flag and having reported the infringement to the Race Committee.

6. An infringing yacht involved in a collision which results in serious damage to either yacht shall be liable to disqualification.

☆ Graduated

1. A yacht which infringes a rule of Part IV may continue racing and complete the course, after which she shall have her Finishing Place in that race adjusted by one of the following Penalty Percents; plus the extra 10% of Section 4, when applicable.

2. The following infringements are assigned Specific Penalty Percents, taking precedence over the General Penalty Percents of Section 3:

a. Infringement of Rule 42.3, the "anti-bargaining" rule 40%

b. Infringement of Rule 42.2(a), "forcing an overlap" at a Mark or Obstruction 40%

c. Infringement of Rule 36 (port-tack yacht keep clear) if, while heading for the line to start or on any windward leg, the starboard-tack yacht is forced to tack to avoid collision; or because of collision 40%

d. Infringement of Rule 44, Yachts Returning to Start; or infringement when the yachts are on different legs of the course 40%

e. Touching a mark, if a rerounding was not properly performed in accordance with Rule 52.2; or if that section is suspended by the Sailing Instructions 20%

f. If the innocent yacht is recorded as DNS or DNF because of collision damage; or because of collision injury to personnel 100%

3. Other than the Penalty Percents specified above in Section 2 and in Section 4 below, the following General Penalty Percents shall apply for infringements of Part IV. The one fact to be determined is whether or not the innocent yacht lost position to the infringing yacht. Position is deemed lost if the infringing yacht crosses ahead; or if she tacks or jibes too close; or if she terminates the overlap in any way other than by dropping clear astern. No position is deemed lost if an overlapping infringing yacht terminates the overlap by dropping clear astern; or if the infringement occurs before the innocent yacht heads for the line to start.

a. Position lost to the infringing yacht 40%

b. No position lost to the infringing yacht 20%

4. If an infringing yacht acknowledges her fault by a reasonably prompt hail (such as "my fault" or words to that effect) and by showing International Code Flag "I" (or such other signal as the Sailing Instructions may specify), the applicable Penalty Percent of Section 2 or 3 shall be used. If fault is NOT so acknowledged, but is later admitted or decided by a protest hearing, then an extra 10% shall be added. The specified signal shall be kept flying by the infringing yacht until she has finished and reported her infringement to the Race Committee.

5. Infringement of a Rule of NAYRU's Part III (General Requirements) or Part V (Other Sailing Rules) may, at the discretion of the Race Committee, be penalized 20% instead of the traditional 100%, provided the infringement did not threaten the safety of any craft or

person; or augment the infringing yacht's speed; or otherwise improve either her position anywhere in the race or her time for completing the course.

6. If there is doubt as to which Penalty Percent to apply, the more severe penalty shall be chosen.

7. The Penalty Percent for an infringement shall be applied against the number of places obtained by subtracting the infringing yacht's Finishing Place from the place for DSQ (one place worse than the number of "Starters" in that race).

8. In calculating the number of Penalty Places: (a) the minimum penalty shall be one place; (b) decimal parts of places shall be rounded off to the nearest whole number; (c) .5 shall be counted as a full Penalty Place.

9. The resulting whole number is the number of Penalty Places to be added to the infringing yacht's Finishing Place, thus obtaining her Adjusted Finish.

10. A yacht infringing during more than one incident in the same race shall have her most-severe Penalty Percent from each incident totalled (but not exceeding 100%) before calculation of her Penalty Places and Adjusted Finish.

11. When penalties are less than 100%, the assignment of Adjusted Finishes shall not affect the Finishing Places of other yachts. (Thus two yachts may receive the same score in a race when one's Adjusted Finish is the same as another's Finishing Place.)

12. If an infringement occurs between yachts of different fleets, the protest rules and/or penalties of the infringing yacht's fleet shall govern.

An example of the Adjusted-Finish calculation:

In a 20-boat race, the 2nd-place finisher committed an infringement that did not cause the innocent yacht to lose position. When the 20% penalty was applied against the 19 places obtained by subtracting 2nd from 21st (for DSQ), the infringing yacht was scored as if finishing in 6th place. The calculation: 20% of $19 = .2 \times 19 = 3.8 = 4$ Penalty Places which, when added to 2nd place, gave the infringing yacht an Adjusted Finish of 6th place.

APPENDIX IV

Limitation of Starters in International Races and Principal National Events

In order to provide good conditions and fair competition, the Permanent Committee of the I.Y.R.U. urges all race committees and sponsoring organizations that are responsible for arranging international races and principal national events to observe one of the following procedures laid down in The Organisation of Principal Events (1973 I.Y.R.U. year book, pages 112-113) regarding the limitation of the number of starters:

(*a*) The number of starters for an international race or principal national event should be limited to thirty boats.

(*b*) Should the number of entries be higher, two cases may occur: either the number in excess is less or more than twenty per cent of the number established above.

Supposing this number to have been established as thirty, if the excess is lower than twenty per cent, a maximum number of thirty-six boats will be allowed to start. If the excess is higher than twenty per cent, competitors will be divided into heats, each heat having approximately the same number of competitors.

(*c*) In the event of a series with an excessive number of entries, the boats assembled will sail elimination races: afterwards a fixed proportion of the best boats ranked will enter the final series (to consist of a minimum of four races), with the scoring to start again at the beginning of the final series.

(*d*) Two examples of elimination series are given for possible guidance, assuming in each case there are ninety entries:

Example (i). The ninety boats are divided into three heats of thirty boats each. Each heat sails the three races without any change in the distribution of the boats. The ten boats best placed in each heat enter the final series, the other boats being eliminated. Scoring in the finals is based solely on the final races, and points for the preliminary races are not taken into consideration.

Example (ii). Obviously, should the entries be ninety, there will be three heats of thirty boats each, should they be fifty, there will be two heats of twenty-five boats each.

Taking the number as ninety, divide the ninety boats in nine groups of ten each lettered A, B, C, D, E, F, G, H, I.

In the first race there will be three heats:—

First heat	A B C
Second Heat	D E F
Third heat	G H I

In the second race the heats will be:—

First heat	A D G
Second heat	B E H
Thirt heat	C F I

In the third race the heats will be:—

First heat	A E I
Second heat	C F G
Third heat	H D B

This does not result in every boat racing against every other boat, but it gets the greatest possible mix. Upon completion of the three elimination races, the thirty boats with the best point scores enter the final races. In case of ties for thirtieth all boats so tied will enter the final races. Those boats not qualifying for the final races will sail in a secondary series.

APPENDIX V

Authority and Responsibility of Race Committee and Jury for Rule Enforcement

The authority of the race committee and jury for rule enforcement is well and clearly established in the rules as follows:

Rule 1.1: "All races shall be aranged, conducted and judged by a race committee under the direction of the sponsoring organization, except as may be provided under rule 1.2."

Rule 1.2: "For a special regatta or series, the sponsoring organization may provide for a jury or judges to hear and decide protests and to have supervision over the conduct of the races, in which case the race committee shall be subject to the direction of the jury or judges to the extent provided by the sponsoring organization."

Rule 1.3: "All yachts entered or **racing** shall be subject to the direction and control of the race committee . . ."

Ways and means of exercising enforcement are provided in Part VI, rules 69 to 73 inclusive, which set up procedures for conducting hearings regarding alleged or apparent infringements, for notifying yachts of such charges and for penalizing infringers. In particular is to be noted rule 73 which reads in part:

Rule 73.1(*a*): "A yacht which fails either to **start** or **finish** may be disqualified without protest or hearing, after the conclusion of the race . . ."

Rule 73.2 "When the race committee:

(*a*) sees an apparent infringement . . .

(*b*) has reasonable grounds for believing that an infringement has resulted in serious damage, or

(*c*) receives a report . . . from a witness . . . not an interested party . . . alleging an infringement,

it may notify such yacht thereof . . . and act thereon . . . as if it had been a protest made by a competitor."

From the quotations and references above, it is clear that the rules provide ample authority to the race committee and jury to enforce the rules and in fact authority beyond that which is ordinarily exercised, while at the same time the rules contain very little which is explicitly directed towards the responsibility which these bodies should assume beyond the deciding of protests. To repeat: "All races shall be judged by a race committee" and "All yachts **racing** shall be subject to the direction and control of the race committee" give the race committee full authority to act on apparent infringements, subject only to the limitations of the procedures established by the rules. It is probably wise that the rules are silent as to the extent to which the race committee is required to initiate proceedings when apparent infringements come to its attention, just as they permit but do not require competitors to lodge protests, but it would seem clear from rule 73.2 that the race committee is expected to initiate proceedings in the exercise of its authority. To what extent should it do so?

It is well accepted that the seriousness of infringements varies greatly, even while recognizing that an infringement, no matter how minor, is still an infringement. An infringement can be so slight that it has no effect what ever on the speed, course or relative position of either yacht; it can be so serious that it results in a collision, disabling both yachts; and it can by almost imperceptible steps be anything between these two extremes. Very few yachtsmen feel inclined to protest a slight infringement that has no bearing whatever on the result of a race. On the other hand, an infringement which involves the risk of serious damage—even if no contact actually occurs—should be, but is not always, protested; nor does the infringing yacht always retire. The same can be said of many other infringements which, while less serious still result in places gained and lost. It therefore is in the best interests of yacht racing that such infringements should result in the retirement, disqualification or otherwise penalizing of the infringing yacht, and that yachtsmen themselves should be encouraged to see that this occurs.

One way to bring about greater observance of the rules is for race committees to institute more proceedings under rule 73.2. Why has there grown up a tendency on the part of race committees not to do so? There are several reasons. For one thing, the race committee feels that it is the prerogative and therefore, the function of competitors to lodge protests. For another, there is a natural disinclination to increase the burden of holding protest hearings. For still another, it is felt that the race committee sees only a small part of the race and why therefore should it call someone to account for something which happens nearby when there may be many other incidents which it cannot see at all? In some instances, too, it feels that since it is to sit in judgment on a case, it should not also be in the position of a prosecutor. But this overlooks the fact that the race committee is an umpire as well as a judge. When a protest is lodged and a hearing held on an incident not seen by the race committee, it performs a judging function in determining the facts and interpreting the rules to arrive at a decision. But when it sees what it believes to be a clear infringement and no protest results, the rules certainly give it authority and somewhat more than an implied responsibility—assuming the infringement is serious and not trivial, and here of course judgment must be used—to take the prescribed steps of rule enforcement. It is, to be sure, recognized that, unlike other sports in which the umpire calls infringements when and as he sees them, the race committee is required to hold a hearing and give the alleged infringer an opportunity to tell his story, but this difference is a difference in procedure, not in function or responsiblity.

The philosophy that in matters of infringements the race committee's function is solely that of judging is sometimes put forward more strongly for the jury, when there is one, than for the race committee itself, but this distinction is not supported by the rules. Rule 1.1 says that "all races shall be conducted and judged by a race committee." Rule 1.2 says the same thing a little differently, in that a jury is appointed "to hear and decide protests and to have supervision over the conduct of the races." Surely the conduct and judging of races includes the right—and the responsibility—to initiate action to enforce the rules. Juries and race committees are expected to be impartial, but partiality is not bringing to a hearing a personal observation of an incident but a desire to favor or penalize one or another competitor. The reason juries are selected for important regattas is not to set up the judging function apart from other functions of the race committee, but to provide as impartial and experienced umpires as possible.

Fully recognizing some of the dangers involved, such as becoming overzealous, race committees and juries should institute hearings under rule 73.2 when there occurs what appears to be a clear-cut and significant rule infringement not protested by a competitor.

☆ APPENDIX VI

A Prescription to Racing Rule 68.4

Protests Involving Measurement and Rating Certificates

General

A protest under the provisions of Rule 68.4 and involving a certificate issued by NAYRU (IOR or CCA Measurement Rules) should be referred to the NAYRU Offshore Administrative Committee by mailing a copy of the protest and the protested yacht's certificate to the NAYRU Offshore Executive Director. The Offshore Administrative Committee will make its decision, and may consult with the NAYRU, ORC, or CCA Technical Committees.

Note that Rule 68.4 *requires* the Race Committee to refer such protests to "an authority qualified to decide . . ." and to "be governed by the determination of such authority." The NAYRU Offshore Administrative Committee is the "qualified authority" for questions regarding the IOR or CCA Rules.

The committee of a one-design class which has the responsibility for measurement and the issuing of measurement certificates is the "qualified authority" for questions regarding that class's measurement rules.

Administrative Protests

In addition to the provisions of Rule 68.4, Administrative Protests concerning Measurement Rules administered by NAYRU's Offshore Administrative Committee may be filed directly with the Committee in care of the Offshore Executive Director.

The Administrative Protest procedure has been established to permit protests of rating certificates at any time after issuance, without regard to whether or not the yacht was *racing.*

Any person or organization which has a sufficiently valid interest in a yacht's certificate may use the Administrative Protest procedure, as follows:

1. The protest must be in writing and shall be dated and signed by the protestor.
2. The protest must include a detailed description of the alleged defect(s) and a full statement supporting a valid interest on the part of the protestor such as owner of a yacht holding a rating certificate, a certified measurer, a Race Committee sponsoring offshore racing.
3. The protest must be accompanied by a copy of the certificate being protested and the current address and telephone number of the owner of the protested yacht.
4. The protest must include a statement of the issue the protestor wishes to have resolved, identification of appropriate Measurement Rules, and other appropriate evidence.
5. A copy of the Administrative Protest and supporting materials must be mailed to the owner of the protested yacht by the protestor.
6. The protest must be accompanied by the Administrative Protest filing fee of $25.
7. The owner of a protested yacht should file a reply with the Offshore Executive Director, in writing, as soon as possible.
8. The Offshore Executive Director will circulate copies of the protest and reply to the members of the Offshore Administrative Committee. The Administrative Committee shall make its decision based on the available evidence and additional evidence it may obtain, and it may order remeasurement of the yacht in whole or part.
9. The Administrative Committee may consult with or refer the matter to the appropriate rule making authority.
10. If the owner of the protested yacht elects to concede the protest or refuses to cooperate in providing for remeasurement, the Executive Director shall invalidate the protested yacht's certificate and so advise all concerned, including the local organization under which the yacht normally races.
11. The decision of the Administrative Committee shall be made as promptly as circumstances permit and shall be communicated in writing to the protestor and protestee.
12. The Administrative Committee shall determine which party will pay and the amount of costs of determining the protest using guidelines as follows:
(*a*) Unless the correct rating of the protested yacht is higher than the protested rating by

more than .2 feet or 0.5% (whichever is greater), the protestor will be responsible for the costs. The $25 filing fee will not be counted towards payment of costs.

(*b*) If the correct rating increases by more than .2 feet or 0.5% (whichever is greater), costs will be borne (or shared) by the owner, the measurer(s), or NAYRU, depending upon the determination of responsibility for the defect. The $25 filing fee will be returned to the protestor.

One-design classes may institute a similar procedure with the appropriate class committee or officer taking the place of the Offshore Administrative Committee.

APPENDIX VII

INTERNATIONAL YACHT RACING UNION RULES

BEFORE N.A.Y.R.U. PRESCRIPTIONS

8—Recalls

1. Unless otherwise prescribed by the national authority or in the sailing instructions, the race committee may allot a recall number or letter to each yacht, in accordance with rule 3.2(*b*) (viii), using yachts' sail numbers or letters when practicable.

18—Entries

Unless otherwise prescribed by the national authority or by the race committee in either the notice or the sailing instructions, entries shall be made in the following form:—

FORM OF ENTRY

To the Secretary .... *Club*
Please enter the yacht .... *for*
the .... *race, on the* ....
Her distinguishing flag is ....
her national letters and distinguishing numbers are ....
her rig is ....
the color of her hull is ....
and her rating or class is ....
I agree to be bound by the racing rules of the I.Y.R.U., by the prescriptions of the national authority under which this race is sailed, by the sailing instructions and by the class rules.

Name ....
Address ....
Telephone No. ....
Club ....
Signed .... *Date* ....
(Owner or owner's representative)
Entrance fee enclosed

24—Life-Saving Equipment

Unless otherwise prescribed by the national authority or her class rules, every yacht, except one which has sufficient buoyancy to support the crew in case of accident, shall carry adequate life-saving equipment for all persons on board, one item of which shall be ready for immediate use.

25—Sail Numbers, Letters and Emblems

2. Other yachts shall comply with the rules of their national authority or class in regard to the allotment, carrying and size of sail numbers, letters and emblems, which rules should, so far as they may be applicable, conform to the above requirements.

28—Flags

A national authority may prescribe the flag usage which shall be observed by yachts under its jurisdiction.

72—Disqualification After Protest

4. The question of damages arising from an infringement of any of these rules or the sailing instructions shall be governed by the prescriptions, if any, of the national authority.

77—Appeals

1. Unless otherwise prescribed by the national authority which has recognized the sponsoring organization concerned, an appeal against the decision of a race committee shall be governed by rules 77, Appeals, and 78, Particulars to be Supplied in Appeals.

2. Unless otherwise prescribed by the national authority or in the sailing instructions (subject to rule 2(j) or 3.2(b) (xvii), a protest which has been decided by the race committee shall be referred to the national authority solely on a question of interpretation of these rules, within such period after the receipt of the race committee's decision, as the national authority may decide:—

(a)   when the race committee, at its own instance, thinks proper to do so, or

(b)   when any of the parties involved in the protest makes application for such reference.

   This reference shall be accompanied by such deposit as the national authority may prescribe, payable by the appellant, to be forfeited to the funds of the national authority in the event of the appeal being dismissed.

3. The national authority shall have power to uphold or reverse the decision of the race committee, and if it is of opinion, from the facts found by the race committee, that a yacht involved in a protest has infringed an applicable rule, it shall disqualify her, irrespective of whether the rule or sailing instruction which led to such disqualification was mentioned in the protest.

4. The decision of the national authority, which shall be final, shall be communicated in writing to all interested parties.

5.(a)   In the Olympic Regatta and such international regattas as may be specially approved by the I.Y.R.U., the decisions of the jury or judges shall be final.

  (b)   Other international regattas shall be under the jurisdiction of the national authority of the country in which the regatta is held, and if satisfied that a competent international jury has been appointed, it may give consent for the decisions of the jury to be final.

6. An appeal once lodged with the national authority shall not be withdrawn.

78—Particulars to be Supplied in Appeals

1. The reference to the national authority shall be in writing and shall contain the following particulars, in order, so far as they are applicable:—

(a)   A copy of the notice of the race and the sailing instructions supplied to the yachts.

(b)   A copy of the protest, or protests, if any, prepared in accordance with rule 68.3(d), and all other written statements which may have been put in by the parties.

(c)   The observations of the race committee thereon, a full statement of the facts found, its decision and the grounds thereof.

(d)   An official diagram prepared by the race committee in accordance with the facts found by it, showing:—

  (i)   The course to the next **mark**, or, if close by, the **mark** itself with the required side;

  (ii)   the direction and force of the wind;

  (iii)   the set and strength of the current, if any;

  (iv)   the depth of water, if relevant; and

  (v)   the positions and courses of all the yachts involved.

  (vi)   Where possible, yachts should be shown sailing from the bottom of the diagram towards the top.

(e)   The grounds of the appeal, to be supplied by either:—

  (i)   the race committee under rule 77.2(a); or

  (ii)   the appellant under rule 77.2(b).

(f)   Observations, if any, upon the appeal by the race committee or any of the parties.

2. The race committee shall notify all parties that an appeal will be lodged and shall invite them to make any observations upon it. Any such observation shall be forwarded with the appeal.

EXCERPTS FROM THE INTERNATIONAL REGULATIONS FOR PREVENTING COLLISIONS AT SEA–1963

(To be replaced in 1976 by new Regulations)

PART B.–LIGHTS AND SHAPES

Rule 5

(b) In addition to the lights prescribed in section (a), a sailing vessel may carry on the top of the foremast two lights in a vertical line one over the other, sufficiently separated so as to be clearly distinguished. The upper light shall be red and the lower light shall be green. Both lights shall be constructed and fixed as prescribed in rule 2(a)(i) and shall be visible at a distance of at least 2 miles.

[NOTE: 2(a)(i) calls for a light "to show an unbroken light over an arc of the horizon of 225° so fixed as to show from right ahead to 2 points abaft the beam on either side."]

Rule 12

Every vessel or seaplane on the water may, if necessary in order to attract attention, in addition to the lights which she is by these rules required to carry, show a flare up light or use a detonating or other efficient sound signal that cannot be mistaken for any signal authorized elsewhere under these rules.

PART D.–STEERING AND SAILING RULES

Preliminary

1. In obeying and construing these rules, any action taken should be positive, in ample time, and with due regard to the observance of good seamanship.

2. Risk of collision can, when circumstances permit, be ascertained by carefully watching the compass bearing of an approaching vessel. If the bearing does not appreciably change, such risk should be deemed to exist.

4. Rules 17 to 24 apply only to vessels in sight of one another.

Rule 17

(a) When two sailing vessels are approaching one another, so as to involve risk of collision, one of them shall keep out of the way of the other as follows:

> (i) When each has the wind on a different side, the vessel which has the wind on the port side shall keep out of the way of the other.

> (ii) When both have the wind on the same side, the vessel which is to windward shall keep out of the way of the vessel which is to leeward.

(b) For the purposes of this rule the windward side shall be deemed to be the side opposite to that on which the mainsail is carried or, in the case of a square-rigged vessel, the side opposite to that on which the largest fore-and-aft sail is carried.

Rule 20

(a) When a power-driven vessel and a sailing vessel are proceeding in such directions as to involve risk of collision, except as provided for in rules 24 and 26, the power-driven vessel shall keep out of the way of the sailing vessel.

(b) This rule shall not give to a sailing vessel the right to hamper, in a narrow channel, the safe passage of a power-driven vessel which can navigate only inside such channel.

Rule 22

Every vessel which is directed by these rules to keep out of the way of another vessel shall, so far as possible, take positive early action to comply with this obligation, and shall, if the circumstances of the case admit, avoid crossing ahead of the other.

Rule 24

(a) Notwithstanding anything contained in these rules, every vessel overtaking any other shall keep out of the way of the overtaken vessel.

(b) Every vessel coming up with another vessel from any direction more than 22½° (2 points) abaft her beam, i.e., in such a position, with reference to the vessel which she is overtaking, that at night she would be unable to see either of that vessel's sidelights, shall be deemed to be an overtaking vessel; and no subsequent alteration of the bearing between the two vessels shall make the overtaking vessel a crossing vessel within the meaning of these rules, or relieve her of the duty of keeping clear of the overtaken vessel until she is finally past and clear.

(c) If the overtaking vessel cannot determine with certainty whether she is forward of or abaft this direction from the other vessel, she shall assume that she is an overtaking vessel and keep out of the way.

Rule 26

All vessels not engaged in fishing, except vessels to which the provisions of rule 4 apply, shall, when under way, keep out of the way of vessels engaged in fishing.

The International Rules apply to vessels on the high seas. The Inland Rules apply to vessels on inland waters including coastal areas.

Copies of the complete regulations, both International and Inland, may be obtained from the United States Coast Guard.

PROTEST COMMITTEE PROCEDURE
in Outline Form

Rules Concerning Protests—68, 69, 70, 71, 72, 73 and 75.
Preliminaries
1. Note on the protest the time it is received.
2. Determine whether the protest contains the information called for by rule 68.3(d) in sufficient detail to identify the incident and to tell the recipient what the protest is about. If not, ask the protestor to supply the information (rule 68.3(f)).
3. Inquire whether the protestor flew a protest flag in accordance with rule 68.3(a) unless rule 68.3(b) applied or the protestor is seeking redress under rule 68.5(a) and note his answer on the protest.
4. Inquire whether the protestor tried to inform the yacht(s) protested against (the protestee(s)) that a protest would be lodged (rule 68.3(c)) and note his answer on the protest.
5. Unless rule 69 applies, promptly notify the protestee(s).
6. Hold a hearing as soon as possible when the protest conforms to the requirements of rule 68 (see 1, 2, 3 and 4 above). Notify the representative of each yacht involved of the time and place of the hearing (rule 70.1).

The Hearing
1. The representative of each yacht involved in the incident is entitled to be present throughout the hearing. All others, except one witness at a time while testifying, may be excluded (rule 70.1).
2. Read to the meeting the protest and any other written statement there may be about the incident (such as an account of it from the protestee).
3. Have first the protestor and then the protestee(s) give their accounts of the incident. Each may question the other(s). Questions by the Protest Committee, except for clarifying details, are preferably deferred until all accounts have been presented. Models are helpful. Positions before and after the incident itself are often helpful.
4. Invite the protestor and then the protestee to call witnesses. They may be questioned by the protestor and protestees as well as by the Committee.
5. Invite first the protestor and then the protestee to make a final statement of his case, including any application or interpretation of the rules to the incident as he sees it.

Decision
1. The Protest Committee, after dismissing those involved in the incident, should decide what the relevant facts are.
2. The Committee should then apply the rules and reach a decision as to who, if anyone, infringed a rule and what rule was infringed (rule 71).
3. Having reached a decision, it should record both the findings of fact and the decision in writing, recall the protestor and protestee and read to them the decision (rule 71).
4. Any party involved is entitled to a copy of the decision (rule 71), signed by the Chairman of the Protest Committee. A copy should also be filed with the Committee records.
N.B. The Protest Committee referred to above may be the Race Committee, Judges appointed for the event in which the incident occurred or a Protest Committee established by the Race Committee for the express purpose of handling protests.

Standard Protest Forms are available from the N.A.Y.R.U. at $1.50 for sets of 25.

RACE COMMITTEE SIGNALS
See Rule 4
AP—Answering Pennant, Postponement Signal

L—Come Within Hail or Follow Me

M—Mark Signal

N—Abandonment Signal

N over X—Abandonment and Re-Sail Signal

N over 1st Repeater—Cancellation Signal

R—Reverse Course Signal

S—Shortened Course Signal

1st Repeater—General Recall Signal

THE
RACING TACTICS

PART TWO

CURRENTS AND WEATHER

If you are in tidal waters, mark on your race circular the direction of current at Start, and when it will change. *(Caution:* Time of current change does not necessarily coincide with printed time of high or low water.)

In beating to windward, favor the tack that will place a current on your lee bow, so current will "push you to windward."

Remember:
Current changes first inshore, last in the middle.
Current runs strongest where water is deepest.
Current runs stronger around a point of land. Look for back eddies behind points of land.
Watch buoys for indications of direction and strength of current.
Give more consideration to effect of current in light airs, less in heavy weather.

Beware of thunderstorms. Be prepared to douse all sail if necessary. But if your course to the next mark permits it, and you decide to take the chance, work over *towards* the storm. You'll get *more* wind. You'll get it *sooner* than your competitors. You may get a *better slant.*

THE START

Signals: N.A.Y.R.U. Rules, Part II, Rule 4

" 2. **Signaling the Course**—The race committee shall either make the appropriate course signal or otherwise designate the course before or with the warning signal. "

" 4. **Signals for Starting a Race**

(a) Unless otherwise prescribed in the sailing instructions, the signals for starting a race shall be made at 5-minute intervals exactly, and shall be either:—

    (i) *Warning Signal*   Class flag broken out or distinctive signal displayed.
    Preparatory Signal   Code flag "P" broken out or distinctive signal displayed.
    Starting Signal   Both warning and preparatory signals lowered.

    In system (i) when classes are started:—

    (a) at ten-minute intervals, the warning signal for each succeeding class shall be broken out or displayed at the starting signal of the preceding class, and

    (b) at five-minute intervals, the preparatory signal for the first class to start shall be left flying or displayed until the last class has started. The warning signal for each succeeding class shall be broken out or displayed at the preparatory signal of the preceding class, or

    (ii) *Warning Signal*   White shape.
    Preparatory Signal   Blue shape.
    Starting Signal for   Red shape.
    first class to start

    In system (ii) each signal shall be lowered 30 seconds before the hoisting of the next, and in starting yachts by classes, the starting signal for each class shall be the preparatory signal for the next. "

Be sure you know whether system (i) or (ii) is being used, since the hoisting and lowering time will differ. Also, in system (ii), the starting signal for each class is the preparatory signal for the next class; in system (i) each class will have its own class flag "or distinctive signal" displayed.

Check your race circular Sailing Instructions, because some yacht clubs vary these.

Also, remember that it is the *visual signal which governs,* "and a failure or mistiming of a gun or other sound signal shall be disregarded." (Rule 4.8).

" 5. **Finishing Signals**—Blue flag or shape. When displayed at the finish, means:—'The committee boat is on station at the finishing line.' "

For complete information see **PART II, MANAGEMENT OF RACES, 4**

There are so many quick decisions to be made before and at the start of a race, that it is wise to eliminate tension wherever possible. One is the question, "What is that signal on the Committee Boat?" Memorize beforehand all the basic signals and flags. Be sure that you have aboard a copy of the race circular with the Sailing Instructions.* Also, a copy of the Racing Rules of the International Yacht Racing Union as adopted by the N.A.Y.R.U. The latter pamphlet, which is easy to stow, gives pictures of the signal flags in color. It may be procured from the Corresponding Secretary, North American Yacht Racing Union, 37 West 44th St., New York, N. Y. 10036, for $2.50 per copy. Team Racing Rules are included.

Rules

" The rules of Part IV apply only between yachts which either are intending to **race** or are **racing** in the same or different races, and, except when rule 3.2(b) (ii) applies, replace the International Regulations for Preventing Collisions at Sea or Government Right-of-Way Rules applicable to the area concerned, from the time a yacht intending to **race** begins to sail about in the vicinity of the starting line until she has either **finished** or retired and has left the vicinity of the course. "

See **PART I, DEFINITIONS—Starting** and **Finishing** (page 42-43).

See **PART II, MANAGEMENT OF RACES, 5** through **13** (pages 48-49).

See **PART IV, SAILING RULES WHEN YACHTS MEET** (page 53-54).

See **PART V, OTHER SAILING RULES** (page 58), particularly **49** through **52, 60** through **64,** and **66.**

Note reference to team racing in rule 49. Also, rule 51.1(d): "Failure of a yacht to see or hear her recall notification shall not relieve her of her obligation to start correctly."

You may be approaching the starting line too soon. If you decide to kill your way, remember that someone may establish an **overlap** to **leeward** with a subsequent right to luff (see rule 40).

Advice

1. Get the Race Circular or Sailing Instructions describing the rules and courses for the race in time to read them thoroughly. Memorize every point which concerns your race.

2. Get to the starting line early. (Some advocate half an hour.)

3. As soon as the course is signalled from the Committee Boat, make sure you know what marks are involved, where they are and whether you are to leave them to starboard or port. Write the course down on the circular.

---

*Appeal No. 66 states: "When a reasonable doubt exists as to an interpretation of a sailing instruction, it must be resolved in favor of a contestant . . ."

4. Plan your race at once with a view to:
The direction of the wind for each leg.
The direction and strength of the currents to be met.
If you are on tidal waters, note the time of tidal change from your tide table, time of current change from current table. Write the time of change on your circular.

5. Put your boat dead into the wind on the starting line to determine which end is favored. Repeat from time to time.

6. Run the starting line from end to end and time the run.

7. Pick the spot from which you want to start.

8. If for any reason you plan to start in the middle (which makes it hard to judge when you cross the line), go beyond the end of the line and get a range down the line onto the shore or on anchored boats to help you as you approach for your start.

9. Start your stop-watches on first signal so that you can check with each subsequent signal. Have someone other than the timer tell him when signals are made. The timer's eyes should be on the watch.

10. Stay clear of the starting area while yachts of other classes, that may start before your class, are preparing to start.

11. Note courses for classes that start before you do. They may help you locate a mark.

12. Check wind indications in all directions as far as you can see.

13. Check competitors' sail selections.

14. Change yours, if necessary.

15. Arrange spinnaker gear.

16. Stay in the starting area during your starting period, (a) to avoid being becalmed too far from line, (b) to learn at once of any course changes.

17. Plan to cross line with maximum speed, or at least with more speed than any competitor to windward.

18. Cross line promptly after your start signal.

19. Cross line with your wind free.

20. Cross line on the *starboard tack* in order to hold right of way, except:
a. When line is laid out at such an angle that all yachts find it an advantage to start on port tack.
b. When there are few yachts and a long line.
c. When arriving so late at the line that there is no possibility of fouling.

21. Practice the kind of start you plan to make:
a. Sitting on the line. Advantageous only for small boats, such as dinghies, where full headway can be rapidly regained. Dangerous if any yacht can overlap you to leeward.
b. Running the line.
c. Running away from your starting spot for a given number of seconds, allowing time for turning, heading back to starting spot. Time for entire maneuver: 1 to 2 minutes for small yachts. (Up to 4½ minutes for largest.) Take a good look at the mark as you come about to see how far away it *looks*.

Windward Starts

A start is a "Windward Start" if the first mark is to windward of your best close-hauled heading; i.e., if you can't fetch the first mark without tacking.

Ideally, the first mark should be dead to windward of the middle of the starting line. But even if your first mark is somewhat to right or left of dead to windward, its location does *not* tell you which is the favored end of the starting line. Reason:

on any up-wind leg you are racing to windward against the *wind*—hence the favored end of the starting line will be the end that is *nearer the wind.*

To ascertain which end of a starting line is *nearer the wind,* head your boat into the wind near the middle of the line and sight abeam in both directions. If either end of the starting line is noticeably to windward of your beam-sight, that end is obviously nearer the wind—hence the *favored end.*

NEITHER END FAVORED

PORT END
FAVORED

STARBOARD END
FAVORED

WINDWARD START: Neither End Favored
WHITE starts on starboard tack at starboard end of line . . .

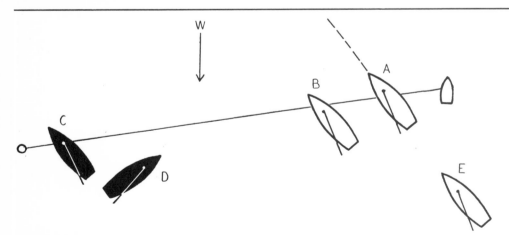

WINDWARD START: Starboard End Favored
A starts on starboard tack at favored end of line (end nearer the wind), is already ahead of C, D, and E. In large fleets, however, many skippers will try to be where A is, causing a traffic jam. Conservative skippers will, therefore, often try to start to leeward of the jam with full headway, as at B, or just behind and to windward of most of the jam, as at E. The best Race Committees don't set this type of line!

. . . holds right of way over BLACK when they meet.

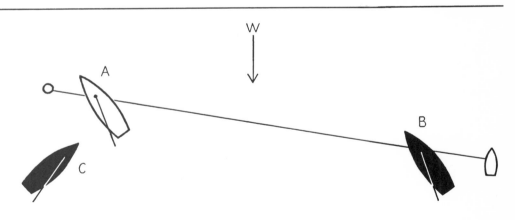

WINDWARD START: Port End Favored
A starts on starboard tack at favored end of line (end nearer the wind), is already ahead of all competitors.

PORT END FAVORED. The Committee Boat end of the line, from which this picture was taken, was apparently the choice place to start.

WINDWARD START: Luffing Tactics

STARTING LINE

Rule 40 has a definite effect on starting tactics. Before the start, BLACK has loafed at the line. WHITE, even though having a very small overlap, can luff BLACK across the line, provided she does so slowly and in such a way as to give her "room and opportunity to keep clear."

Before *and after* the starting signal WHITE cannot luff BLACK "above a close-hauled course," unless her mast is forward of BLACK's helmsman. (Read Rule 40.)

Therefore, it is now advisable for BLACK to loaf *at least two lengths* behind the line. This will give her room to respond to WHITE's luff without having to cross the line. Being to leeward of boats at the line can now be an advantage rather than a handicap. By luffing them you can also free your wind.

FREE STARTS: Wind Forward of Beam
(A start is a "free start" if you can sail free toward your first mark, i.e., not close-hauled.)

The gun is about to go. WHITE arrives at the line ahead of BLACK and back-winds her. As leeward yacht, she has right-of-way. After the starting signal she must not deprive BLACK of room at the mark either by heading above the first mark or by luffing above close-hauled. When clear of mark she luffs BLACK.

Advantages of windward end of line: Yacht nearest mark has wind clear. If she is up with the gun, she may blanket other yachts. She sails a freer course to first mark—important on a close reach.

Disadvantages of windward end: Crowding and consequent danger of fouling or being blanketed. If early, she cannot kill time by bearing off on yachts to leeward, and if she luffs she may end up on wrong side of mark. If late, she may be backwinded. If Committee Boat is at windward end, there is danger of being blanketed.

FREE STARTS: Wind Abeam
WHITE, leeward right-of-way yacht, makes every effort to cross line ahead of BLACK (above) so as not to be blanketed. Backwinds BLACK, luffs her up and . . .

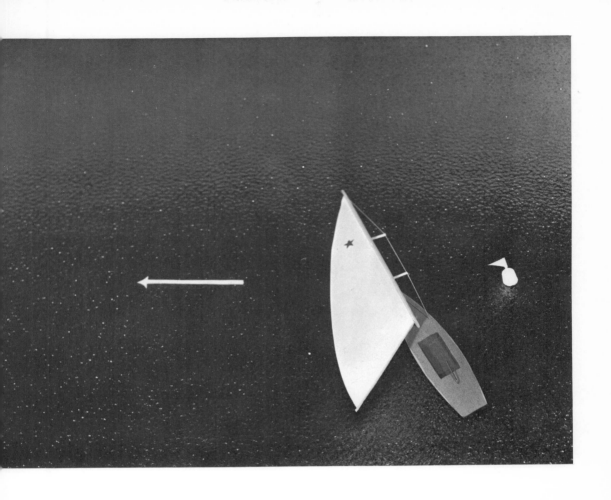

. . . starts for first mark on a faster course (wind high on beam) than BLACK at windward end of line.

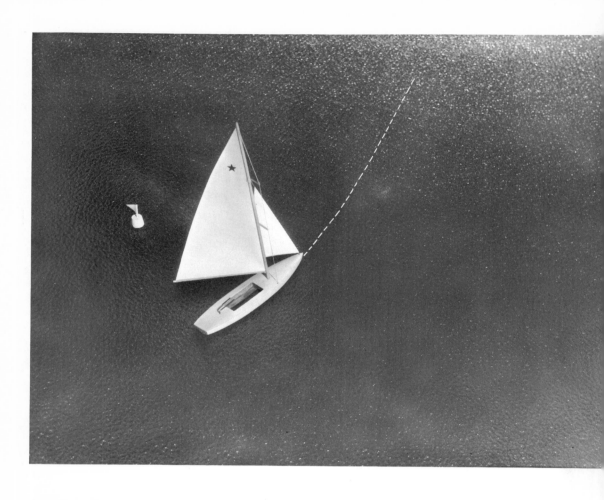

FREE STARTS: Wind Abaft the Beam
WHITE (above) starts at leeward end of line, if that end is clear of other yachts
and far enough away not to be blanketed by yachts to windward at other end of
line. Travels slightly faster course to mark or . . .

. . . WHITE (above) tries for extreme windward position, luffs slightly after start and blankets BLACK.

FREE STARTS: Wind Astern

If the first mark is at no great distance from the starting line, choose the end of the line which will give inside position in rounding first mark. Otherwise start at the end of the line (in this case the left) which will give you a faster sailing angle to the first mark.

Or, make a late start so as to be able to blanket other boats. Do not set spinnaker or whisker pole until after crossing line, in order to keep boat free to maneuver.

ADVANTAGE of the leeward end of the line. The Star in the foreground is killing time while waiting for the gun. If she hardens up in time, she will be out ahead travelling fast and with her wind free of the jam at the windward end.

TO WINDWARD

TACTICS

Tack as little as possible but consider a quick tack after start to clear your wind.

Unless you are in a desperate position at the rear, don't tack away from the fleet when their course is the logical one. The percentages are against your gaining by it.

Watch what the best skippers are doing.

If your yacht has a compass,* check your heading on each tack for possible headers† or lifts.†

When you get a lift, stay on that tack. When you get a header, come about.

Other things being equal, always take the tack that takes you more directly to the mark.

* Beware of deviation if your boat has *iron* keel.
† See Glossary.

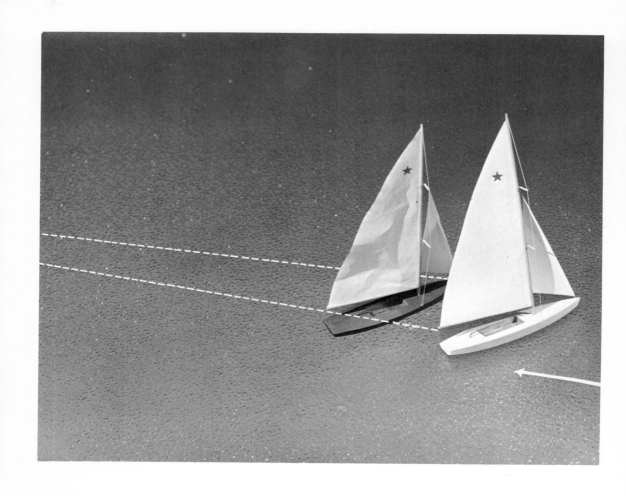

BLANKETING (On Beat to Windward)
Wind shadow of WHITE extends 4 or more mast lengths to leeward, tapering to a
point. The distance depends on strength of wind and size of yacht.

BACKWINDING (On Beat to Windward)

Left: Wind strikes WHITE's sails and is deflected in such a way that BLACK cannot point so high. It also disturbs air flow on lee side of her sails. Right: In this position BLACK is in difficulty not only from backwinding but she is also held back by the disturbed water of WHITE's wake.

Gray indicates extent of arc affected by backwind on a beat to windward.

BACKWINDING (On Beat to Windward)
Left: It is even effective when yachts are abeam, but if WHITE, the leeward yacht, drops behind even a little she will be affected by BLACK's wind shadow. Right: Backwinding is particularly effective from this position. By trimming her mainsail flat, WHITE can increase the degree of deflection of the wind.

SAFE LEEWARD POSITION. Notice the shape of the two mainsails and the angle of inclination of the two masts.

GOING THROUGH to leeward. The three pictures were taken within 30 or 40 seconds in about a 12 knot wind.

1. DEFENSE—Single Competitor

1. Single Competitor Close: When in the lead, the general rule is to cover your competitor by tacking whenever and as soon as he tacks. WHITE is ahead. She covers BLACK on every tack.

2. Single Competitor at Some Distance: If yachts are far apart, WHITE tacks to cover BLACK at such point that she will be directly to windward of BLACK:

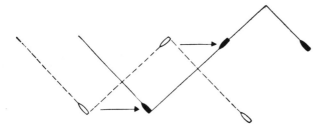

2. DEFENSE—Several Competitors

WHITE has good lead (longer than is suggested in model diagram on facing page) over several competitors. She chooses a course half way between courses of her competitors, only leaving this course to cover whichever boat seems to be over-hauling her.

3. DEFENSE—In the Lead, Competitor Pointing Higher
WHITE finds BLACK is pointing higher, perhaps due to a better wind.

Before it is too late WHITE tacks so as to put BLACK in her wake.

4. DEFENSE—In the Lead and to Leeward
WHITE is ahead but to leeward. She tries to work carefully up to windward . . .

. . . even sacrificing speed and distance ahead, in order to put BLACK in her wake.

5. OFFENSE—Breaking Through to Leeward
If it is not practical for WHITE to split tacks and if she is unable to work up to
windward of BLACK, she may try breaking through to leeward, even at the cost
of losing ground to windward.

She bears off and with increased speed runs through narrow part of BLACK's wind shadow, then makes every effort to work up to windward, being less handicapped now by reason of being clear of wake and backwind. With a good boat, superior helmsman and luck, she may make it.

6. OFFENSE—Splitting Tacks

WHITE splits tacks repeatedly while BLACK tries to cover her. On each split WHITE gains, since BLACK does not know the exact moment when WHITE will tack and consequently makes more abrupt turns and thus loses headway. WHITE finally gains "safe leeward position."

7. OFFENSE—When on Port Tack

WHITE has approached BLACK on port tack. If WHITE is a small yacht and maneuvers easily, she can go about close to leeward of BLACK *provided her bow will be ahead of* BLACK *after she has filled away and resumed speed on starboard tack.* She will then be in "safe leeward position" and able to backwind BLACK. (See above.)

Even if WHITE had been far enough ahead to cross BLACK's bow and blanket her, she would have to be careful not to allow BLACK to pass to leeward while she was regaining speed after tacking.

8. Tacking to Windward Alone
Left: In going into a windward leg do not make a short tack first. There is danger that you will misjudge the time to tack and may overstand the mark. Right: Correct. Make long tack first. Make short tack when abeam of buoy.

Note: Throughout the book, considerations of tide and current are omitted.

REACHING

TACTICS

Keep your wind clear.

Beware of luffers.

Avoid trying to pass close to windward of a persistent luffer, if being luffed will endanger your position in relation to other yachts.

Try to pass well to windward (or to leeward) to avoid being luffed.

Maneuver to be inside at the mark.

If there's doubt as to whether you should set your spinnaker, and the skipper just ahead of you elects to hoist his, attack to windward while he is hoisting.

1. DEFENSE

WHITE counters every windward move by BLACK, holding her astern in zone of backwind and disturbed water, but keeping in mind that if BLACK steers a course to pass to leeward, WHITE must not sail "below her proper course." (See rule 39.)

2. OFFENSE—Breaking Through to Windward

WHITE luffs at favorable moment to faster sailing angle than wind abeam, breaks through point of intersection of BLACK's bow and stern waves, and passes about a mastlength to windward.

If BLACK should counter every move, and WHITE is only a short distance behind, WHITE would threaten first to windward, then to leeward, repeating this until an opportunity arose to break through.

3. OFFENSE—Breaking Through to Leeward

From position in picture at top, WHITE works off to leeward toward end of BLACK's wind shadow. Before reaching it WHITE heads up to bring wind forward of abeam, the fastest course.

With added speed, due to this course, she breaks through wind shadow and tries for "safe leeward position."

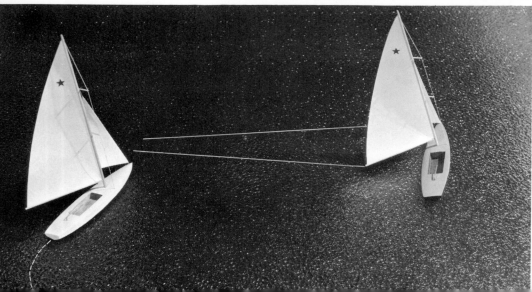

BEFORE THE WIND

TACTICS

Keep your wind clear.

Consider advantages of staying to leeward.

Play your spinnaker every minute.

Avoid prolonged luffing matches.

Plan ahead for inside position at the leeward mark.

ADVICE

With wind astern, put weight sufficiently on side opposite boom to heel boat and thus ease pressure on tiller.

When wind is puffy, bear off in gusts; sharpen up as wind lightens.

BEFORE THE WIND. Jib vs. Spinnaker.

1. OFFENSE—Passing to Windward
WHITE follows closely in BLACK's wake . . . blankets her . . .

128

. . . and passes to windward. Entire maneuver should be so timed that BLACK does not have time to blanket WHITE before WHITE reaches finish line or next mark.

Next mark, dead ahead, to be left to port. To be sure of inside position at mark, WHITE slows down, drops back, heads up to faster sailing angle across sterns of competitors . . .

. . . blankets them, establishes an overlap before BLACK is within "two of her overall lengths of the mark," gains inside position . . . and (below) rounds first.

3. DEFENSE—Luffing

BLACK starts to blanket WHITE. But WHITE luffs so sharply that . . .

. . . BLACK cannot pass to windward. WHITE bears away, holds lead.

If luffing match is prolonged to the point where both yachts will have to jibe in order to head for the mark, WHITE should jibe *first* if mark is to be left to starboard, and WHITE should jibe *simultaneously* if mark is to be left to port.

WHITE wishes to cross in front of BLACK in order to gain inside position at mark. She follows course indicated, sacrificing distance while blanketed, but gaining position. WHITE can be sure of succeeding only if she leads BLACK by *at least two lengths.*

ROUNDING THE MARK

RULES

" 51—Sailing the Course "

" 2. A yacht shall sail the course so as to round or pass each **mark** on the required side in correct sequence, and so that a string representing her wake from the time she **starts** until she **finishes** would, when drawn taut, lie on the required side of each **mark. "**

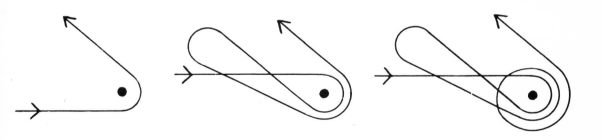

Left: Correct rounding, mark left to port. Center: Error made and unmade, but mark not yet rounded correctly. Right: Error made, unmade, and mark rounded correctly. "String," when drawn taut, will lie on required side of mark.

" 3. A **mark** has a required side for a yacht as long as she is on a leg which it begins, bounds or ends. A starting line **mark** begins to have a required side for a yacht when she **starts.** . . . A finishing line **mark** and a finishing limit **mark** cease to have a required side for a yacht as soon as she **finishes.**

4. A yacht which rounds or passes a **mark** on the wrong side may exonerate herself by making her course conform to the requirements of rule 51.2.

Rounding Mark Alone

Course A is correct. Yacht loses a minimum of way. Yacht following this course can cut inside yacht following course B, will not kill speed as would yacht on course C. C might at times be necessary as a competitive maneuver if other yachts are close and next leg is to windward.

When rounding a leeward mark, and the next leg is windward, make most of your turn *before* you reach mark so that you can pass it close aboard and harden up at once.

Avoiding an Extra Tack

Left: WHITE cannot quite make mark. Maintains full headway without pinching until last minute, then uses way to carry her around buoy. Right: BLACK tries to pinch and make buoy, loses speed and is forced to tack.

1. DEFENSE—Overlapped at the Mark

BLACK has slight overlap on WHITE at leeward mark. WHITE must give room.

WHITE allows BLACK just enough room and no more, thus attaining "safe leeward position." Course A would have put WHITE in BLACK's backwind.

Because WHITE, owing to proximity of BLACK, cannot swing wide before rounding, she stays to windward in approaching mark and makes sharp turn, sacrificing headway in tight turn in order to be to windward on next leg.

3. DEFENSE—Covering After Passing Mark

WHITE is closely pursued at leeward mark. Next leg is to windward. Shall she remain on same tack or come about? WHITE points high on same tack until BLACK rounds mark and comes about to clear her wind. WHITE tacks immediately and covers.

If WHITE had had a substantial lead she would have remained on same tack for half her distance ahead, then tacked, thus putting herself dead to windward of BLACK and able to cover effectively on either tack.

4. OFFENSE—Approaching Mark on Starboard Tack
WHITE approaches windward mark on starboard tack. BLACK, on port tack, must give way.

In large classes, whenever a windward mark is to be left to *port, approach it on starboard tack.* However, when mark is to be left to *starboard,* case shown below illustrates how a yacht on port tack, with proper timing, can outmaneuver starboard tack yacht.

WHITE, port tack, times approach to mark so as to pass astern of BLACK, starboard tack, and round mark ahead of her, since BLACK, *while tacking,* must keep clear of WHITE.

5. OFFENSE—Winning Windward Berth After Rounding
WHITE swings wide before rounding mark in order to be to windward of BLACK
on next leg.

GLOSSARY

ABAFT, towards the stern.

ABEAM, the direction at right angles to the line of the keel or centerboard.

AFT, towards the stern.

AMIDSHIPS, usually in the line of the keel, but sometimes midway between bow and stern.

ANCHOR-RODE, anchor rope.

ASTERN, CLEAR (see page 6).

BACKWIND, the wind deflected from its natural course by a yacht.

BARGE, to force one's way contrary to rules, between another yacht and a starting mark.

BEAM, see Abeam.

BEAR OFF, to alter course to leeward.

BLANKET, when yacht gets the windward berth, taking wind from the other's sails, the latter is said to be blanketed.

BOOM, a spar at the foot of a fore and aft sail.

CLOSE-HAULED (see page 5).

COUNTER, the after part of a yacht's hull where the lines converge towards the stern; the underside of the stern overhang.

COVER, for a yacht in the lead to duplicate tack for tack the maneuvers of a following yacht.

DISQUALIFIED, ruled out of a race.

FETCH, in close-hauled sailing when a yacht arrives *at or to windward of* a given point or object.

FOUL, a breaking of the rules.

FREE, a yacht is sailing free when not sailing close-hauled (see Close-hauled) and not in the wind.

FULL AND BY, when all sails are drawing (full) and the course is as close to the wind as possible.

HEADER, a sudden wind shift toward the bow.

HELM, the tiller.

HULL, the main structure of a yacht.

JIBE, to swing off before the wind to the other tack, the boom shifting itself, sometimes violently.

LEEWARD, towards the lee (see page 5).

LEG, the course from one mark to another.

LIFT, a sudden wind shift away from the bow.

LUFF, to alter course more nearly into the wind (see page 4).

OVERLAP (see page 7).

POINT (higher), sail closer to the wind.

PORT, the left side of a yacht.

REACH, a tack with the wind abeam, forward of the beam or abaft the beam.

RIGHT OF WAY, the right to proceed on one's course.

RUN, sailing with the wind astern.

SHARPEN THE WIND, to come more into the wind.

SHEET, a rope used to control a sail.

SHEETS STARTED, sheets eased beyond the point of being close-hauled.

SPARS, a term applied to all masts, yards, gaffs, booms, etc.

STARBOARD, the right side of a yacht.

STAYS, IN, headed dead into the wind and not filled on either tack.

STEM, the foremost timber in a yacht.

TACK, (a) a course sailed with the wind on one side of a vessel. A vessel is on the port tack if the wind comes over the port side.

(b) to go about by going into the wind is to tack. (See page 4.)

(c) The lower forward corner of a fore-and-aft sail is known as the tack.

WAKE, the track of a yacht left astern.

WAY, a yacht's movement through the water.

WIND, ON THE, sailing close-hauled.

WIND, IN THE, headed into the wind.

WIND-SHADOW, the path of dead air in the lee of an object.

WINDWARD, the direction from which the wind is blowing (see page 5).